EFFECTIVE

COMMUNICATION

SKILLS

How to Talk to Anyone.
A Practical Guide to Boost Your
Conversation and Writing Skills in
the Workplace, Improve Charisma
and Build Healthy Interpersonal
Relationships.

Dalton McKay

Table of Contents

Page left intentionally blank

Introduction

Communication is a skill and a science that mostly involves talking and connecting. Beyond these traits, communication is also a non-verbal language. The more you improve your communication skills, the more comfortable you will be in sharing your thoughts and opinions. This greatly improves your self-esteem as you begin to realize that communication is natural, universal, and not to be feared.

Communication allows us to express how we feel, what we think, and what we know. Using verbal and non-verbal language to successfully communicate, we are able to gain new knowledge and share what knowledge we already have. Being able to share what you know or feel with others allows you to build fulfilling and lasting relationships.

Fluent communicators possess a certain set of skills that you can analyze and mimic to improve your own ability to effectively communicate. There are a few questions you can ask yourself as you study fluent communicators and before you actually practice their skills. For example, is it possible for one to become successful in communicating with *all* types of people? Or, how can one conquer their anxieties related to communicating with others?

Effective communication starts with someone having an idea, learning something new, or otherwise holding onto something they yearn to share with someone else. Once they have the intention to share the information, they will then choose what mode of communication to utilize based on the person they are telling, the environment they are in, and any other considerable circumstances.

The ideal model of communication chosen will be the one that enables you to get your message across properly. If the person you are talking to has received your message the way you intended for it to be received, then you have effectively communicated. Additionally, for communication to be effective, it is important for you to choose a mode of communication that does not inadvertently distort the message or its purpose.

Ultimately, the mode of communication you choose to use in any given circumstance is crucial to ensuring your message is received properly by the recipient. Few things are as frustrating as trying to communicate something to someone and failing to do so in such a way that they are able to understand you. This is why it is important to learn about different modes of communication—what they are, when they are most effective, and how to apply them to your life.

Chapter 1: Communication - The Basics

The basic elements of communication are as follows:

The Sender – This is the person who seeks to share information they hold with someone else. For example, a teacher might learn new information while away at a teaching conference and return to class with the intention of sharing this information with their students.

Message – This is the feeling, idea, request, or any other form of specific information that the sender has in mind and would like to pass on. Referring to our previous example, the message in this situation would be the information gathered while away at a teaching conference— let's say, a new useful book that was published related to the class material.

Encoding – This is the very moment when the sender converts the idea or the thinking into actions, words, diagrams, or any other manner that will drive the idea into the message.

Ultimately, the sender will have knowledge of their recipient to be able to choose the best way to reach them.

Media – This is the type of route or medium that the converted idea and message is conveyed to the intended party. Media can take many forms, including but not limited to face-to-face communication, television, art pieces, e-mail, letters, and many others. For example, the teacher will most likely use face-to-face communication to share with her students the new book she discovered as teachers in traditional classrooms use this media most often.

Decoding–This is the process of translating the message from the best way you are able to understand it to the best way the recipient of your message is able to understand it. If the teacher is teaching a 5th-grade classroom, they would ideally communicate their message in such a way that a 5th grader could understand.

Receiver – This is the individual or group of individuals that the message is being sent to. In our example situation, the students would be the receivers. There can be one receiver of a message (i.e. a direct text message to a friend) or millions of receivers of a message (i.e. political campaign).

Feedback – This is basically the reaction that the receiver will give in response to the message that was sent to the receiver by the sender. For example, the response that the students will give to the teacher about the new book—let's say strong eye contact, which might indicate that they are interested—would be the feedback.

Noise – These are the obstacles that hinder the communication process and directly impact how the message is delivered and received. For example, a lack of concentration by the students when the teacher is talking about the new book is the "noise" that will most likely hinder this particular instance of communication. Another example would be if the teacher decided to share the conference information with the students at the end of the day, when students are most likely tired or ready to go home.

Types of Communication

There are four fundamental categories that detail the most common types of communication used.

Verbal Communication: This method relies on words to communicate something. This is the standard way of communicating. The majority of people use this type of communication on a day-to-day basis. However, sometimes we use it without fusing it with other types of communication. Tone, motions, and non-verbal communication are just a few different things that people use while passing information to one another. Observations, feelings, and opinions can be best communicated through verbal means. A conversation via the phone, catching up with a friend, or displeasure conveyed are mainly done verbally. It is easier this way for most of us.

When we were still children, we grew and learned verbal communication by listening and imitating the sounds around us. In a short while, we could understand languages and prompted us to speak verbally while growing. Verbal communication is additionally isolated into four portions:

Intrapersonal Communication: Intrapersonal communication consists of private talks that we have with ourselves and we, generally, keep this to ourselves. There is the possibility, however, that we inadvertently communicate what we did not wish to due to our body language, facial expressions, or other nonverbal cues.

Relational Communication: This is a one-on-one kind of conversation where two people have to be sharing or holding a conversation. Relational communication is mutually beneficial—both individuals are senders and receivers of information, and both are able to understand one another well.

Small-Group Communication: This type of communication takes place when more than two people are involved. The number of individuals will be just enough that effective communication can still occur. Question and answer sessions, work meetings, and psycho educational groups are a perfect example of this kind of communication. Unfortunately, miscommunication can arise in small groups, especially if the topics at hand allow room for disagreement. For example, a question and answer session might become heated if someone answers a question in such a way that half of the group understands and agrees, and half of the group does not understand or agree.

In a typical organization, communication happens in the following ways:

Chain Flow of Communication: This is when someone who holds a "higher-up" position at a company needs to communicate a message to subordinates but cannot do so directly. Instead, they communicate it to the position just beneath them, who then communicates that message to the position just beneath them, and so forth. The message eventually gets to the workers who need to hear it, but because it was passed on so many times, it is often received as skewed or inaccurate.

By now, you might be asking yourself if chain flow of communication is such an unreliable mode of communication, why do organizations continue to use it? Below are a few examples of when a superior might need to utilize chain flow of communication to send a message to subordinates:

- Giving observations and criticism on how work has been done.

- Issuing work guidelines, corporate policies, and so forth.

- Giving a complete rundown to the workers on what is required of them in order for the organization to hit ion ts targets.

- Communicating the organization's strategic vision or mission statement to every worker.

- Brochures, e-mails, and so on are examples of written chain flow of communication. For effective and error-free communication, the superiors should:

- Indicate the main objective as clearly as possible.

- Guarantee a precise message, explicit and unambiguous.

Upward Flow of Communication: This is the kind of communication that is designed for a particular goal in an organization. Its objective is to inform the progress of the firm. The lower offices make use of this kind of communication to address issues and ideas to the offices above them.

Subordinates also use this method to inform the bosses on how well they understood instructions from them and to seek clarification on issues that are not clear to them.

This type of communication process is designed to ensure the company is successful and creates faithful and committed employees, as it is important for workers to be able to have a voice within their place of employment. The bosses are made aware of the workers' feelings towards their directives, work, and the whole company at large.

Upgraded systems, suggestions and complaints boxes, and work reviews are some factors that collaborate to make this type of communication a success. Reports about the position of the organization, as well as reports on studies conducted in the company that are drafted by the employees and other external professionals also help this type of communication to be more effective.

Parallel Communication: This is the kind of communication that takes place at the same level within an organization. This could look like communication among coworkers, among supervisors, or among CEOs—each of these groups communicates with others of the same work or professional status. The benefits of this type of communication are:

- Efficiency.

- Encourages positive challenges within the company.

- Gives real-time social collaboration to the individuals.

- It helps handle issues when they arise.

- It assists in the sharing of information.

- It can be utilized for finding solutions after disagreements between offices and individuals.

Diagonal Communication: This is the kind of communication that takes place when executives and representatives meet up. It doesn't show up on a hierarchical outline. For instance, the budget planning of the organization or a specific branch or office under the organization, and auditing of the funds.

External Communication: Communication that takes place between someone who works directly with a company and someone who is not at all associated with that company. For instance, suppliers, banks, credit facilities, and so forth. The objective could be either to plan how the two organizations could work together in the future or any work that will benefit both companies.

Open Communication: This kind of communication takes place when one single person communicates messages to groups of people who attend with the intention of receiving those messages. Political rallies and religious gatherings are perfect examples of this specific kind of communication. In this instance, information is transferred from one source to the others who are voluntary receivers of the information.

Non-Verbal Communication: This is a communication type that does not rely on words or sounds. It is the opposite of verbal communication. This kind of communication uses gestures, body language, facial expressions, and any other communication that does not rely on verbally spoken words. Non-verbal communication could be viewed as a supplementary form of communication when used in conjunction with verbal communication.

Visual Communication: This type of communication incorporates the use of pictures or videos to transmit information. To understand the message being sent, one has to see the visual guides that are being showcased. For example, photos, signs, images, print outs, and maps are a few of the mediums that are used in visual communication. Movies, plays, and video television programs are the best in communicating visually. Visual communication can as well include information exchange as content electronically through telephones and computers. An Emoji can also be classified as a type of visual communication.

At the time when symbols are utilized, they assist the reader and clients in understanding their importance in communication. The best example of this type of communication is definitely the Web, which has a number of characteristics with a mix of pictures, words in shadings, and different fonts as well as graphs. These visual highlights demand us to see the screen and process the information to understand the message.

Media communication is creating at a transient rate to guarantee lucidity and to take out any uncertainty. The previously mentioned four categories of communication have assumed a fundamental job and keep on doing as such, in crossing over any barrier between individuals, trade, training, social insurance, and amusement.

Written Communication: This kind of communication contains noteworthiness that is useful in different communication platforms. This communication is key when planning and executing a business module, as it helps improve data storage. In any case, writing can be unique in both formal and informal styles. The best kind of writing is when every factor of the writing has been considered before starting, and all the correct wordings are put to use. Another positive aspect to consider, is that writing is more dependable when it comes to getting your point across. The message doesn't have an opportunity to change. The writer is forced to put together a complete thought before attempting to communicate.

It has the following advantages:

- Written communication assists in putting down to paper the standards, principles, and rules that an organization uses in its operations.

- It is a perpetual method for data sharing and comes in handy where records and documentation are needed.

- It sets down the exact job descriptions where references could be made, unlike verbal communication, where one could easily forget and does not have a point of reference.

- Written communication is precise and to the point.

- Well written communications can uplift the company's standards as compared to other organizations.

- It gives readily available records for reference.

Written communication has some downfalls, as well, that include:

- Written communication is costly as it entails too much paperwork and money to send the documents to the desired goals.

- Replies and feedback from written communications are not instant as compared to other forms of communications.

- Composed communication is tedious, and reactions not prompt. The writing and sending require more than just time but also money.

- Effective written communications call for more knowledge and fluency in the language as well as understanding, as poorly written communications are prone to misinterpretation.

- A lot of administrative work and message weight is included.

Composed or written communication is the type where words and sentences are used together to enable information to be passed on. Journals, diaries, phone text messages, organizational reports, magazine and newspaper articles are some examples. In contrast to other types of communication, composed messages can be corrected by the sender right before they are sent to the recipient making this an important factor in communicating both in official and casual circumstances. This type of communication outweighs other types, such as visual communication, especially when using electronic mediums; for instance, PCs, telephones, and other visual mediums such as televisions.

Communication Barriers

There are many reasons why all types of communication, regardless of the know-how and means of sending, may encounter barriers that slow the process. In numerous circumstances, the message may be misinterpreted by the receiver and hence not be the original information that the sender had intended to pass along. Listening, paying attention to, and understanding a message helps to receive the message without any changes, but the sender and receiver should acknowledge that there are powerful barriers to communication.

At any stage of communication, the information may encounter these barriers. Boundaries may alter the message, and one has to dedicate a great amount of time and resources in correcting that. Compelling communication includes beating these boundaries and passing on an unmistakable and clearly expressed message.

Some typical boundaries to proper communication include:

Language that contains special terms within a specific field, commonly known as Jargon. - A critical factor to question before utilizing language is, "Who is the receiver of my message?" If you are a master at addressing another authority in your general vicinity, language might be the ideal approach to communicate something specific while manufacturing expert security—like how closest companions can convey in code. For instance, a data innovation (IT) frameworks investigator speaking with another IT representative may utilize language as a method for sharing data in a manner that fortifies the pair's shared information. In any case, that equivalent discussion ought to be held in Standard English, free of language, when speaking with staff members outside of the IT gathering.

Emotional obstructions and taboos – The passionate atmosphere during the meeting may still make another mental hindrance to successful communication. Outrage, antagonistic vibe, or doubt can mutilate both the sending and accepting of implications. Such feelings may make us veil or exaggerate our actual sentiments. Our worry winds up winning as opposed to communicating. The more grounded such emotions are, the more uncertain that a successful trade of understanding will happen.

Distraction with different issues can cultivate negative sentiments that structure a communication problem. Non-verbal communication may show sentiments of impassion, restlessness, insignificance, or negligence to the next message, adding to the problem.

Frames of mind can be a significant hindrance to powerful communication. How we feel about the message, the recipient, or even ourselves influences the tone and exactness of the message. On the off chance that we disapprove, we have an "it-can't-work" or "smarty pants" approach, endeavors at communication may end up being just simply making an insincere effort. If we accept that all government officials, sales reps, or individuals from an ethnic gathering are similar, any message we get from them will be influenced by our opinion rather than fact.

As a relationship advances, there is an expanded propensity to share data, dispositions, and conclusions. Be that as it may, camouflage of data through equivocation, compliancy, or forcefulness happens when there is a relationship of doubt.

Lack of attention in some situations or when we encounter some interruptions, can take away our concentration. For instance, an explorer may focus on one "NO PARKING" sign but is unable to pay the same kind of attention to multiple signs that could erect across the city. In this way, dull messages ought to be overlooked for powerful communication. This can also be seen in an office set up where a worker does not pay attention to new instructions and assumes them to be the normal ones, then proceeding with the usual routine.

Contrasts in recognition and perspective – Semantics are the implications individuals connect to words. The various associations individuals relate to a similar word makes one hindrance to powerful communication. It has been proposed that words are just images that allude to something. Since we see reality through our arrangement of channels, the implications we dole out to these images of reality may vary from the effects others relegate to them.

They may likewise bring out passionate reactions that lead to misconception. "Love mother hound," "wild," "water rights benefit" may evoke various pictures for various individuals and diverse, intriguing gatherings.

Pick words for our messages that reflect reality as we see it through our channels. Depending upon how we see another, we may depict that person as "mindful," "weak," "kind" or "delicate;" a similar individual might be portrayed as "liberal" by the individuals who favor him and a "squanderer" by the individuals who don't.

The point when communicators appoint various implications to similar words, connections become contorted, and the message ends up being misjudged by the recipient or recipients.

This is when you can't "come out with the simple truth of the matter." You can just say how you see it.

Individuals with physical incapacities, by and large, are unfortunate with regards to picking up work. They have been underestimated since the beginning of time with the exception of some cultures, and this can make them have low confidence and experience social uneasiness, ultimately hindering their success in their jobs and life.

It can make a physically tested individual have to face troubles in self-divulgence and have negative effects on their social lives.

Physical obstructions to non-verbal communication – While evaluations of the measure of data imparted non-verbally go as high as 90 percent, a look into these studies shows that we are not genuinely adept at recognizing non-verbal signs.

Rosenthal, professor of English Literature at the University of Wales, directed a survey of non-verbal communication tests and finished up individuals' speculations concerning non-verbal signs that are not exact. In an analysis they led at the University of Houston, oil organization arbitrators saw videotape accounts of 30 speakers. The mediators at that point appraised the speakers as fair, sly, or misleading. The outcomes: the moderators' exactness extended from as low as 27 percent right to a high of just 43 percent right. Further, the mediators were similarly as sure of the precision of their wrong decisions as they were of their right ones. The arbitrators felt generally few of their decisions were even somewhat dubious.

Language difference and the trouble in understanding new accents – Recognition is commonly how people understand their surroundings. People do better with understanding a message if the idea is noteworthy to them. Be that as it may, any message that is poor quality will not be understood regardless. An equivalent example could be, an individual is on leave for a month because of personal reasons. The Human Resource Manager may be unsure if they should keep the individual or get a substitution for them, so the effectiveness of the company does not go down.

Desires and wrong judgment may prompt false presumptions. People will always want to hear what they hoped the message meant and not the actual meaning of it. "A man hears what he needs to hear and ignores the rest."- Simon and Garfunkel's recognition is a mental obstruction to communication. Our minds continually get numerous messages. However, we can only deal with each in turn. In this way, we select the significant messages and set aside the rest. For instance, we shouldn't know about the sentiment of our left shoe except if there is an issue with it. In this way, more often than not, we screen it out. So also, we screen out immaterial clamors.

We may likewise screen out messages or parts of messages that don't accommodate our view of the real world. We shut out inadmissible data and select just those things or realities that fit our thought of what should be. Anything that goes against our beliefs is very difficult to accept.

Additionally, we tend to screen out messages as indicated by our needs at a specific time. We select the message we find most relevant right then and there. On the off chance that too many messages are coming in, communication over-burden results, and none of the messages may get past. This is why it is important to organize your schedule and give ample time to receive communication.

Choosing just certain components from a message, we change the message's importance.

Social kinds of contrast - The limits of people working and conversing together change instantly when communication is done in a certain type of way. For instance, the right to have personal space is not even across all societies.

A well-equipped individual in the society who is trying to share messages and communicate with the peers should be privy to this kind of information so that they are keen on the understanding of their message in the society. It is crucial to take into consideration who you are talking to and what is culturally and socially accepted by that person.

Barriers in Communication by Category.

Language Barriers: Clearly, language in different settings may play a big role as a boundary to communication. With that noted, the choice of words when communicating in a similar language might be in itself confusing and hinder the receivers of the message from understanding the initial meaning that was intended to be passed along. For instance, a message that incorporates a great deal of pro-language and condensing won't be comprehended by a collector who is curious about the wording utilized. Medical officers are more prone to this kind of mistake. It is therefore advised that when communicating, one should use the type of language that the recipient will understand.

Physiological Barriers: Physiological boundaries are a result of a person's physical state at a particular moment. For instance, a deaf person may not fully understand the message directed to them verbally as they cannot hear what the sender of the message is putting across.

Physical Barriers: This is typical when there is a geographical separation between the receiver and the sender while they are communicating. Communication is normally easy and timely, as not much technology or resources are required to enable the process of passing information. Albeit current innovation frequently serves to diminish the effect of physical boundaries, the points of interest and goal for every communication from both the sender and receiver should be visible to beat the physical barrier between the two.

Attitudinal Barriers: Attitudinal obstructions are practices or discernments that keep individuals from passing on information fluently and uninterruptedly. This barrier may be caused by a lack of inspiration, poor administrative skills as well as interpersonal clashes. To achieve an effective communication channel, the individuals with this kind of barrier have to change from within first, encouraging the flow of communication.

Mental Barriers: The condition in which the receiver of a message is mentally will act as a barrier to how they will understand the information conveyed to them. For instance, if somebody is stressed over something that they are thinking about at a particular time, it could make them not understand fully the message given to them as their concentration is not on the message but on the issues at hand. Stress can also play a major part in affecting personal relations.

Being hot-tempered could cause obstruction to communication. When furious, it is hard to control the wording that we use, and hence, the recipient has a hard time understanding the message. Individuals with low self-esteem might be less decisive, and because of this may not feel great imparting - they may be shy to express themselves or even shy to read some messages.

If you are interested in improving your self-esteem, I wrote a book on the subject that you can find on Amazon. Go to the last page of this book and you will find the direct link.

Overcoming Barriers

There are a lot of barriers to communication in recent years. The recipient does not well understand the message sent by the sender and hence, there is a breakdown in the flow of effective communication. It is fundamental to get solutions to having the barriers around during interaction, to achieve a more successful and effective communication.

The following are tips on how to overcome significant boundaries of communication.

Killing contrasts in recognition: An organization has to confirm that it has employed the exact people who fit the jobs. There has to be a doable program that works to achieve the big objective of the company. This can be achieved by having training days for the employees to sharpen their communication skills.

Utilization of simple word arrangement to understand language: Use of straightforward and clear word arrangement while communicating is key. Arrangements of words that are hard to understand should not be used.

Decrease and disposal of commotion levels: Noise is the prime communication boundary in every medium and should be reduced at all costs. It is fundamental to recognize the source of the distraction and, after that, wipe out that source.

Undivided attention: Listen carefully and cautiously. There is a big difference between listening and hearing. Undivided attention means while paying attention, one is still able to understand what they are hearing. By posing inquiries, the speaker can decide whether the recipients have understood the message.

Enthusiastic state: While communicating with one another or in a group kind of set up, one should not express what they feel about the message being presented by their fellow correspondent. This will ensure the continuous delivery of the information from the sender. For instance, on the off chance that the delivery of the message is feeling off, at that point, the other correspondents may imagine that the data being presented to them isn't true.

Straightforward organizational structure: The structure of the organization should be easy to understand. Progressive levels in the organization ought to be realistic and there should be a perfect range of control inside the association.

Evade information overload: The person or persons who are delivering the information should realize how to organize their work in order to minimize too much unnecessary information. The energy of planning and executing tasks should be organized in a careful manner to achieve more output from the employees using the least amount of resources.

Give constructive feedback: The outcome of a conversation may not be pleasing, but all in all, it has to be conveyed in a calm manner. Helpful input will prompt effective communication between the bosses and employees. Constructive feedback can result in an understanding between individuals and a more successful work environment.

Legitimate media selection: The employees should choose the right kind of media to assist in marketing that passes information to their target recipients. Messages should be passed on orally, as well as with up close and personal collaboration or gatherings. Making use of this kind of medium can assist the organizations in passing the information more clearly for the recipients to easily understand it. A written method of communication could also be used to convey important messages such as notices, memos, and so on.

Adaptability in gathering the objectives: Work in an organization should be arranged in a manner that every single employee is working to be able to achieve the greater organization objective, and this is made possible when the instructions are given in an effective way from the one creating the message. When direction is given, it should be given so that every employee can both grasp and relate to the message so that a universal understanding is created.

Remove Filters

This is the act of retaining data to deal with a particular individual response. The familiar saying, "Don't kill the messenger!" outlines the inclination of receivers for situations where information shared at a workplace was not directed from the boss to be plain and clear for all of the employees. A guardian who doesn't go along a total message is actually filtering the information. For example, an employee may erase emails that contain useful data for the organization; hence, filtering data even before it shows up.

It is obvious that filtering can cause a lack of knowledge to the organizations' employees by denying them a chance to inform themselves about a particular issue as well as the current state of the organization. To beat filtering, it is advisable that information is sent numerously to the receiver using more than one medium of communication. By doing so, the barrier of a message being filtered will be reduced. For example, the message from the boss could be sent by both email and a printed copy attached to the information board.

Individuals will, in general, channel bad news more during upward communication; it is likewise useful to recall that those beneath you in a company might be careful about sharing bad news. One approach to defusing the situation with representatives who unmistakably pass on data upward is paying little respect to whether the news is good and bad.

Media rationalist Marshall McLuhan claims we experience life by watching it through our goggles and arrangement of images. The pictures of reality we see are shaded, changed, and separated through these goggles. These pictures go through and are twisted by various channels, including our encounters, our instruction, and our dispositions. Thusly, no two individuals append similar importance to a mutual occasion.

In a typical communication procedure, the sender's choice of medium to use while sending a message is influenced by specific factors that play a big role while the message is being formed. The sender's feelings, encounters, instruction, qualities, and generalizations (about the message or the recipient) will, in general, be consistent channels. Others, for example, the sender's state of mind at the time the message is passed on, may shift extensively now and again. The sender's channels impact how the person in question communicates the message - which words, signals, and voice tones to utilize.

The message being sent to the receiver should follow a similar medium if it is to reach the recipient. The receiver mode of receiving the message dictates how they will actually understand the message. The two arrangements of channels in communication twofold the possibility for misconception. Monitoring your channels and your capacity to conform to them, both as a sender and a collector, is significant for diminishing the odds of miscommunication. A compelling communicator additionally considers the beneficiary's channels and endeavors to encode the message so the recipient can decipher it with ease.

Here is a portion of the criteria that people may utilize when choosing whether to carry a message or pass it on:

- Does the receiver prefer the notion that "no news is uplifting news?"

- Does the Sender's fear any unplanned disappointments that would hinder them from sharing information?

- Is the situation within his domain of skill, providing room for them to actually translate the message correctly, or would he say that it is beyond their skill set to understand the message's true meaning?

- Does the message contain essential information that the receiver may require?

By and by, sifting can prompt miscommunications in business. Every audience interprets the message into their very own words, making their very own form of what was said. (Alessandra, T., 1993, Communicating at work. New York: Fireside).

We send our messages through both verbal and non-verbal channels. The verbal sign is the expressions of the message, the substance. The words we pick are dictated by our jargon, our channels, and our appraisal of the collector's capacity to get them. The non-verbal sign transmits the social component of the message. Our stances, body developments, contacts, manner of speaking, eye to eye connection, stops, the pace of discourse, and volume all show how we feel about the message, how we feel about ourselves, and how we feel about the collector.

Non-verbal conduct has a more grounded effect on impressions than going with a verbal message. Assessments of the measure of importance passed on through nonverbal messages keep running from 60 percent to 90 percent. The more passionate the message, the more importance is relegated to the non-verbal segment. At the point when the verbal message and the non-verbal message are not consistent, we, as a rule, accept the non-verbal message.

The recipient's understanding is the significance the collector gets from the sender's message. The importance might be actually as the sender planned, or it might be mutilated to some variety of the aim as it goes through the channels and different carriers of the message. The viability of communication is a proportion of how intently the recipient's understanding matches the sender's goal.

Feedback is the beneficiary's affirmation that the message has been received. It might be verbal, non-verbal, or both. The best input goes past, recognizing that the message has been gotten. It tells the sender how it has been received and what significance the recipient made of it. Criticism additionally goes through the two arrangements of channels. In this way, similar to the first message, it is dependent upon change.

This criticism makes successful communication a two-way process. Two-way communication requires more exertion than a single direction, yet it lessens the odds for misconception between people.

Chapter 2: Effective Oral Communication

The 7%-38%-55% Rule

In communication, a speaker's words are just a small amount of his endeavors. The tone, speed, and mood of his verbally expressed words, and the pauses between those words may express more than what is being conveyed by words alone. Further, his motions, stance, posture, and articulations more often than not pass on an assortment of different signs. These non-verbal characteristics can give an audience significant hints on information regarding the speaker's musings and sentiments and, in this way, prove the truth of the speaker's words.

The most normally cited study on this matter is one by Albert Mehrabian, Professor Emeritus of Psychology at the University of California, Los Angeles. During the 1970s, his examinations proposed that we overwhelmingly tend to reason our emotions, frames of mind, and convictions about what somebody says not by the genuine words verbally expressed, but by the speaker's non-verbal communication and manner of speaking.

The truth, Prof. Mehrabian evaluated this inclination: words, manner of speaking, and non-verbal communication separately represent 7%, 38%, and 55% of individual communication.

As a matter of fact, when a speaker's words together with their non-verbal communication contrast, audience members are bound to accept the nonverbal communication of the speaker, not his words. For instance, if an individual states, "I don't have an issue with you!" while evading eye to eye connection, looking restless, and keeping up a shut non-verbal communication, the audience will likely confide in the predominant type of communication, which as per Prof. Mehrabian's discoveries is non-verbal (38% + 55%), as opposed to the strict significance of the words (7%.)

In my opinion, there are two possible objections that can counter an overly simplistic interpretation of "Rule 7-38-55". First of all, it is not easy to understand how much the paraverbal and non-verbal language on the effectiveness of communication counts. And then, these quantifications are very subjective and cannot be applied universally to any context. The same Prof. Mehrabian has warned us about this.

Non-verbal components are especially significant for communicating emotions and frame of mind, particularly when they are incongruent: if words and non-verbal communication differ, one will, in general, accept the non-verbal communication.

Indicated by Mehrabian, the three components account diversely for our preference for the individual who advances a message concerning their sentiments: words represent 7%, manner of speaking records for 38%, and non-verbal communication represents 55% of the enjoying.

When talking about powerful and significant communication about feelings, these three pieces of the message need to help one another - they must be "consistent." If there should arise an occurrence of any incongruence, the beneficiary of the message may be disturbed by two messages originating from two unique channels, giving prompts in two distinct ways.

The accompanying model should help show inconsistencies in verbal and non-verbal communication. "I don't have an issue with you!". The individual keeps away from eye to eye connection, looks on edge has a shut non-verbal connection, and so on.

It turns out to be more probable that the beneficiary will confide in the dominating type of communication, which to Mehrabian's discoveries is the non-verbal effect of tone+gestures (38% + 55%), as opposed to the exact importance of the words (7%). This is known as "the 7%-38%-55% Rule".

It is imperative to state that in a separate investigation, Mehrabian led examinations managing communications of emotions and frames of mind (i.e., like-hate) and that the above mentioned, lopsided impact of the manner of speaking and non-verbal communication winds up convincing just when the circumstance is vague. Such vagueness shows up for the most part when the words verbally expressed are conflicting with the manner of speaking or non-verbal communication of the speaker (sender).

Below is a diagram illustrating the 3 divisions:

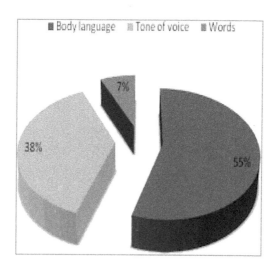

The "7%-38%-55% principle" has been generally misjudged. It is frequently guaranteed in any communication that the significance of the

information is passed on mostly by the use of non-verbal prompts and not through the importance of words. The speculation from the - at first unmistakable states in his analyses is the normal misstep made in connection to Mehrabian's standard.

This examination is a helpful—if not exact— update that nonverbal prompts can be more important and telling than verbal ones. Along these lines, to be viable and convincing in our verbal communication — in introductions, open talking, or individual communication — it is basic to supplement our words with the correct tone and voice and the fitting non-verbal communication.

Communication Styles

The work by Dr. Eileen Russo is shown beneath. It demonstrates that two distinct measurements in communication styles are present: the degree of how to express oneself and the degree of emphatics.

Every image speaks to an alternate communication style. Individuals can fall anyplace inside every quadrant, fusing up consistently more than one particular style over the others further from the mid-point. Take note that more emphatic communication styles tend to dictate to others what to do. While the less decisive communication styles tend to request of others what ought to be finished.

The most expressive communication styles will, in general, demonstrate their feelings outwardly, discourse, and tone. The less expressive kind will choose to either not express their feelings or work on them. Below you can find the four fundamental communication styles. In the accompanying segments, we'll take a gander at the fundamental attributes of every communication style and a few things you can do to help your communication well with each sort.

Spirited Communication Style

The spirited communication style is keen on a 'master plan.' Those who use this style are the visionaries, the creators, and the pioneers in the gathering. Their communication might be brimming with fantastic thoughts and exaggerations that will, in general, be influential to others from the start.

They are not, in every case, truly adept at talking about subtleties and tend to make stories seem more fantastic then they may seem. It is common for people who are spirited communicators to go off on tangents.

Their composed verbal communication may tend to sound more sensational. While they can be exceptionally engaging, getting them to convey plainly on specific points may take the help of another person to direct them through a discussion and keep them on track by taking them back to the current subject.

Tips on how to relate and communicate if you use a spirited style:

- When thinking about new plans to share, likewise think about whether you have recommendations on the most proficient method to place those thoughts into activity.

- Respect settled upon plans that have been set to run meetings.

- Try to restrict sharing individual stories that will sway off the subject of the discussion.

- Be sure to enable others to share their thoughts and recommendations while at the same time, you are tuning in.

- Be sure any solicitations you make are clear, and any inquiries are open to being made.

- Share your gratefulness for other individuals who have put forth work and effort.

Tips on how to relate with individuals with the spirited communication style:

- Use motivation with time breaking points recorded for every subject.

- Praise them before other individuals.

- Learn to divert the discussion back to the current subject delicately.

- Understand that they may misrepresent.

- Challenge them to separate their' huge thoughts' into precise results and steps.

- Agree to assist where you can in what they are willing to partake in.

- Use registration or other composed updates as a way to help convey what should be finished.

Examples of Spirited Communication Style:

When speaking with somebody who is spirited, it may be challenging to try and keep them on the subject at hand. What's more, when you have their attention, keeping it is another issue entirely. You will find that consistency is essential while speaking with spirited individuals. If you can get them used to a specific arrangement or strategy for communication, it will be simpler to keep them focused and engaged. This doesn't mean continually picking email over choosing the phone just because it is their preference. However, it means regularly utilizing follow-up inquiries or monitoring a standard premise to check whether you are both still in agreement.

Here's a case of a decently composed communication to a spirited individual.

'Hello there, Sally!

I thought your introduction yesterday was awesome! I delighted in the manner that you had the group of spectators take part in the session.

I figure you would be an extraordinary decision for the instructive segment at our next executive gathering. The Board of Directors needs some data about nearby financial patterns, however, in a way that isn't too exhausting or convoluted.

Would you prefer to talk about this over lunch? I'm free on Thursday or Friday this week. Fill me in regarding whether both of those days will work for you.

Much appreciated!

George'

For what reason would this communication work for a spirited individual? It is energetic, integral, and would complement Sally. She will be satisfied that you saw her first introduction and increasingly confident that you might want her to rehash it.

Of course, you're sure to have an exceptionally energized individual on your hands at lunch. So be ready. You could bring a diagram of the points you need to cover in the introduction. Request her info and ensure you've arranged sufficient opportunities to let her give it. At that point, help her lay the thoughts down and note them for her. Sending a subsequent email or note will help guarantee that you are both on a similar page also.

Keep in mind, the spirited individual is valuable for every one of their abilities and every bit of excitement, so with a little structure around your interactions, you can be successful in communicating without smothering the very characteristics they bring to the table.

Direct Communication Style

As demonstrated in the communication style grid, individuals with a direct communication style are profoundly decisive and not expressive. They will, in general, instruct others as opposed to asking others what they think ought to be done, and they won't effortlessly indicate feelings in their communications with others. Their communication style is intended to be practical. However, others may not always see it that way. They may seem brisk and cold to other people, who may think about their style of communicating literally.

This style will let others know exactly how they feel before proceeding onward to the following subject, not because they are attempting to be shifty, but because they are trying to spare time. They won't generally stop to tune in to other people, regardless of whether the others have something significant to contribute. They may appear to be restless and domineering now and again, yet it's not intended to be received that way.

They are trying to concentrate on results as opposed to feelings. They will express their real thoughts, regardless of whether it could be off-putting to other people. Try not to anticipate that they will discuss their own lives–they like to keep business and individual issues isolated. They don't give up and on occasion, could be viewed as being forceful as opposed to decisive due to the manner that they express their assessments.

Tips on how to communicate while having a direct communication style:

- Always listen completely to other people and abstain from hindering.

- Create time for 'talking' toward the start of a gathering.

- Allow others to express their feelings about points.

- Recognize that conceptualizing can be useful and not only a 'period squanderer.'

Tips for communicating with people with direct communication style:

- Ask on the off chance that they have the opportunity to talk before hopping in.

- Be straight forward and don't exhaust them with loads of background data.

- Limit 'visiting' or discussion that is off-theme.

- Be direct with your communication.

- Request a particular source of inspiration or make a specific solicitation.

Examples of Direct Communication Style:

When speaking with somebody who has the immediate communication style, the key is to get to the primary focus of your communication as quickly as time permits and to do so in as productive a way as would be prudent. The principal model underneath demonstrates the kind of communication that won't work with somebody who has a direct communication style. In this model, Jane is the one with the direct communication style.

'Hello there, Jane,

I got notification from Alex that you handled another huge business account yesterday. He said that you worked superbly in disclosing the organization's advantages to the client and that you were extremely proficient.

Alex additionally said that the client requested a statement on another telephone framework for his current workplaces.

Have you pondered how you will continue? Fill me in regarding whether I can help you to get the statement together or on if you need or would like to hear any thoughts on the setup.

I'd like to get the statement to the client the in the not so distant future, on the off chance that you want to oversee it. That way, we would have a decent possibility of getting the request in during the current month's numbers.

Anne'

'Jane,

Incredible job on the new account. I'd like to meet for 10-15 minutes tomorrow to talk about methodology and timing. It would be ideal if you informed me as to whether you'd want to meet at1:00, 1:30, or 2:00 pm.

Much obliged to you,

Anne'

See the distinction? The first does in the long run, get to the heart of the matter. However, it is too close to home sounding and doesn't give an unmistakable question for the individual to react to. This example still conveys a complimenting message and asks a question, yet it does as this in a much clearer manner. If it appears to be brief to you, don't stress, the direct style individual will value it. It's a superbly proficient form of communication, and there is considerably less of a possibility that the reader will not understand.

For instance, suppose Mary and Greg, a married couple with two little children, are encountering a snapshot of pressure because of an absence of communication. She is feeling overwhelmed with handling clean up and sleep time obligations, while he wants to snooze after supper. Mary could without much of a stretch bottle her frustrations and become progressively disappointed with Greg's absence of assistance, in a roundabout way communicating everything that needs to be conveyed through snorts, glaring looks, and exasperated moans. Or on the other hand, she could go up against the issue head-on utilizing direct communication, which may happen like this:

Mary: "I'm feeling overpowered by cleaning the kitchen and putting the children to bed each night. How might you feel about taking on the kitchen tidy up?"

Greg: "If it's alright with you that I rest directly after supper when I generally feel that I need it, I'd be happy to clean the kitchen after I wake up."

Systematic Communication Styles

This is a type of communication for an individual with a precise style that likes to concentrate on reality and subtleties as opposed to possibility and conceivable outcomes. They hope for the receiver to utilize and acknowledge the rationale when the message has been received. They will acknowledge facts as opposed to the '10,000-foot view' thoughts that have not yet been demonstrated. These thoughts are seen as unhelpful.

They might be slower to react to your communication, as they are presumably examining the circumstance and building an intelligent, very much considered reaction. Outlines, charts, and patterns are, for the most part, valuable devices for speaking with systematic communicators also.

Those with a systematic communication style are awkward with communicating their sentiments about things and don't care for confrontation. They may, in general, shut down communication as opposed to managing enthusiastic or angry circumstances. In the event that you need to have this type of conversation, you should be careful and exact in describing your emotions to them.

The more data you can give them, the more joyful they will be. The length of the data is relevant and written communication can be the right way to go about this. Having a concrete log of important data is always the way to go, especially when it comes to business.

Tips on how to communicate if you have a systematic style:

- Accept that not every person pursues straight points of view and basic leadership.

- Encourage good working connections, thought and other people's emotions are significant.

- Exercise to pose qualifying inquiries that will enable you to get the data you need.

- Always make inquiries concerning others in the event that you need to assemble affinity.

- Make sure you comprehend the extent of an undertaking with the goal that you don't sit around gathering data that won't be required.

- If you have to request more opportunities for investigation, have the option to clarify the advantage of the data you are dealing with.

Tips for communicating with people with a systematic style:

- Be keen on the realities of the circumstance instead of people's suppositions.

- Speak with exactness and precision as opposed to speculations.

- Plan your moments well when you speak with them.

- Give coherent purposes behind your activities and for what you ask of them.

Example of a Systematic Communication Style:

When you have to speak with an individual who has a systematic communication style, recall that realities are what to underline. Sentiments won't be extremely powerful. Utilize legitimate, straight reasoning, and impart similarly. Step them through your reasoning, don't bounce in front of any details. It will spare you time if you set aside the effort to clarify your contention or musings through the first run through.

In the event that you need a systematic communicator to settle on a choice, let information do the talking for you, as much as could reasonably be expected. Have outlines? Know a few patterns? Have guides to demonstrate how something functions? These can be valuable in speaking with a precise individual. On the off chance that you are trying to urge them to help with a thought that isn't upheld by the information, you will be in for somewhat of a test. Be that as it may, you can at present get their assistance if you are able to clarify your position sensibly.

Keep in mind too that systematic kinds are not inclined to imparting individual data to work partners.

You shouldn't think about this; literally, it's basically what they like. However, in the event that they do propose an individual topic with you, you can, as a rule, take it to dole out that they feel increasingly comfortable.

Considerate Communication Style

Found in those individuals with this considerate communication style are significant worries about what others think or feel. They need to satisfy other individuals and to be incorporated into their companion's gathering. They like to work with others, help other people, and interface with the individual explanation level. On the off chance that there is a confrontation at your gathering, they are bound to try and intervene.

They need everybody to get the opportunity to express their real thoughts, have their turn, and collect acknowledgment for their commitments. They are regular coaches and instructors and appreciate helping other people succeed. They will support a bunch of coordinated effort and communication; however, they are not constantly pressured to talk about their own personality traits.

This is a significant communication challenge for those with this chivalrous character style – they might be hesitant to impart a contradicting insight, regardless of whether it's substantial data, since they are worried about keeping the harmony and being enjoyed.

They are additionally disposed to accept direct communication as an individual issue. It's hard for them to isolate other people's' suppositions about a subject from their own feelings, and thus may feel that a specific conclusion is expected or others will dislike them. There is additionally the likelihood that they will be talked into something to safeguard the harmony as opposed to holding fast to their own convictions.

<u>Tips for communicating if you have a considerate communication style</u>:

- Understand that not every person pursues direct manners of thinking and basic leadership.

- Realize that good working relationships are achieved by allowing other individuals to express themselves.

- Exercise to ask qualifying inquiries that will enable you to get the data you need

- Ask other inquiries concerning themselves in the event that you need to manufacture affinity.

- Be sure you comprehend the extent of a task, so you don't sit around idly gathering data that won't be required.

- If you have to request more opportunities for investigation, have the option to clarify the advantage of the data you are taking a shot at.

Tips for communicating with a person with considerate style:

- Focus on the realities of the circumstance as opposed to people's sentiments.

- Speak with exactness and precision as opposed to speculations.

- Organize and schedule points when you speak with them.

- Give sensible purposes for your activities and your requests.

- Permit time for research before conclusions.

- Personal topics are to be avoided unless the conversation is open.

Examples of the Considerate Style of Communication:

To best speak with somebody who has this type of communication style, recollect that the individual's sentiments will be significant. They will listen best when you make them feel as though their emotions are important to you, their assessment is imperative to you, and that you value them as a colleague and person. This doesn't mean that you need to be genuinely expressive yourself; however, appearing as fascinating to them as an individual will go far.

Why not begin your communication with a question about how their kid is getting along, or how their last vacation was? This little bit of your time can have an extraordinary return. In the event that you have something to impart that will maybe be seen as a basic, you should step circumspectly so as to be powerful. Tell the individual that you value their work and name the perspectives that you discover essential and significant.

At that point, note the progressions that should be made, clarifying the purpose behind the changes as much as you can. Grin, and utilize open non-verbal communication to tell them that there is nothing personal about what is being said. At any conceivable moment, use demands rather than goals in examining the required changes.

For considerate style individuals, using an example to address an issue rather than being direct is a great one to use when being cautious. It works to the point effectively, it shows care for the other individual, and it makes questioning an act more acceptable.

But there's another point of view, a different way of seeing communication styles...

Every individual has a communication style that they use to relate to others.

To understand the characteristics of these styles, it is best when we separate them into four styles.

Passive Communication - A style wherein people have built up a body language and tone of not communicating and sharing their emotions, sentiments, and even addressing their needs. Thus, they do not react well to anger or outrage prompting instances. Rather, they allow for complaints and displeasure to add up, generally ignorant of the development hence affecting their tone and body language. Yet, when they have arrived at their high resilience edge for unsatisfactory conduct, they are most likely to explode with bitterness, and that causes bad relationships with people around them. After the incident, be that as it may, they may feel disgrace, blame, and perplexity, so they return to being aloof.

Passive communicators will regularly:

- Not affirm for themselves.

- Always create space for other people to take advantage of their privileges.

- Do not take time to express what they feel about different circumstances and also their personal feelings.

- They will be keen on how they speak so as not to make conflict with others.

- They do not show attentiveness while communicating with others.

The effect of an example of aloof communication is that these people:

- They at all times, feel to be out of place.

- They are discouraged as they feel to be in a state of misery.

- Regularly feel unhappy as to them it appears that their needs are not being taken care of.

- They frequently do not accept their current state of emotions.

- Personal development is rare as they believe their problems do not attract any attention for help.

A passive communicator will behave like:

- "I can't go to bat for my privileges."

- "I have no idea what my privileges are."

- "Everybody is looking down on me."

- "I'm weak and cannot help myself."

- "No one cares about my emotions."

Aggressive Communication - This is a type of communication that individuals damage other people's privileges just by the way they put across their ideas and proposals. In this manner, aggressive communicators are verbally as well as physically damaging.

Aggressive communicators will regularly:

- Always want to rule and head others.

- They tend to use embarrassing words to enable them to control others.

- They look down on others.

- they are harsh to others.

- They hardly get disappointed.

- They talk in an arrogant manner when making requests.

- They use threats when dealing with others.

- They hardly listen to other people's sentiments.

- Always try to hinder other's progress.

This kind of communicator will tend to behave like:

- "I am always right, and you are wrong."

- "I am bossy, and I like it."

- "I can get rid of you when I want."

- "I am able to cut all the privileges."

- "I am able to pick myself up."

- "I don't need you."

- "It's everything your missing."

- "I respond in a split second."

Passive-Aggressive Communication - This is the style where individuals seem to be not so caring about everything going on around them, but they work on the issues when alone, and no supervision is available. This is the type of individual who tends to build up examples of aloof forceful communication but, at the same time, feel angry, stuck, and feeble. They believe in not being equipped fully to handle particular situations. They, therefore, express their displeasure by unpretentiously undermining the article of their feelings of disdain.

Passive-aggressive communicators tend to:

- Murmur things to themselves other than taking up challenges.

- Always notice issues that they strongly dislike.

- They make use of the wrong appearance instead of working on the right one.

- Big fans of mockery.

- Hard to accept reality.

- Tend to behave like they are assisting, but in reality, they are not as helpful as they seem.

- Utilize harm to get even.

An example of passive-aggressive communication is that these people:

- Do not have a nice relationship with the people around them.

- Stay stuck in a place of feebleness (like POWs)

- Do not develop as they do not work on existing problems.

The passive-aggressive communicator will say things like:

- "I'm frail and angry, so I damage, baffle, and upset."

- "I'm too frail to manage you head on, so I should utilize passive communication."

- "I will seem agreeable; however, I'm most certainly not."

Assertive Communication - This is a style where individuals openly express their assessments and sentiments and solidly fight for their rights and needs without damaging that of others. These kinds of individuals esteem themselves, their time, furthermore, their enthusiastic, profound, and physical needs and are solid go-getters as they achieve in getting what they believe is theirs while not spoiling that of others.

Assertive communicators tend to:

- Not be afraid to state what is theirs in a straightforward manner.

- Express their emotions obviously, and consciously.

- Use "I" proclamations.

- Convey other people's rights too.

- They are keen to listen.

- They are responsible for their own actions.

- They are attentive when communicating.

- Talk in a polite and unmistakable manner.

- They have a casual lifestyle.

- They have good relationships with others.

- Feel equipped and ready to take charge.

- They do not give others the chance to control them.

- Go to bat for their privileges

The effect of this type of communication is:

- They feel well connected with others.

- They are responsible for their actions.

- Develop quickly as they are quick to pinpoint issues as soon as they come up.

- Create an environment for others to develop and develop.

The self-assured communicator will say, accept, or carry on such that says:

- "We are also qualified deferentially to each other."

- "I am sure about who I am."

- "I understand I have options, and I take time to pick."

- "I talk with care and to the point."

- "I am not in control of others but myself."

- "I believe my privileges should be considered."

- "I am in control of my needs."

- "I respect the privileges of others."

- "No one owes me anything unless they said so."

- "I'm fully in charge of my own progress."

Self-assuredness is what makes an individual or breaks them as if it guarantees good emotions and the well-being of stable connections.

Remember that a large portion of us don't utilize an assertive communication style in each association; they're just ways that you can use to convey. When all is said and done, assertive communication is destined to prompt aware and longer-term connections, with the goal that allows the style to make progress much of the time.

Nonetheless, passive-aggressive communication may work better on certain events. For instance, when feeling scared that you are going to be hurt, passive communication may defuse the circumstance, and aggressive communication may keep the issue from deteriorating. While the passive communication style can be useful, when individuals pair it with inconspicuous animosity, the passive-aggressive style is probably going to meddle with or undermine solid connections.

Nine Steps to Effective Listening

In the present cutting edge, rapid, high-stress world, communication is more significant than ever, yet individuals appear to commit much less time to truly listening to each other. We tend to be doing too many things at once. Smartphones have made this a real issue and people are now up against social media, internet searches and constant over communication and stimulation.

Veritable listening is now regarded as a blessing as it is hard to get one's attention. Listening has a lot of advantages such as resolving disagreements, mending relationships, clearing up misunderstandings, among many others. At a job set up, effective listening ensures fewer mistakes made. Also, direct and understandable instructions for the seniors while at home, listening can help create a family that moves in one direction in harmony.

Step 1: Maintain eye contact.

In the world now, eye to eye connection is seen as a key element to show that one understands what is being communicated to them. While talking, it is advisable to maintain eye contact by setting aside all manner of interruptions for maximum concentration. Maintain it regardless of whether they are doing the same back to you. Some social setups will not approve this as they are linked to different feelings as well as taboos, but it is good to reason out with the receiver of information and at the same time, don't divert away from the topic.

Step 2: Be attentive but relaxed.

Try not to be occupied by your own thoughts, emotions, or inclinations. Allow the speaker their time so they can complete their sharing of information. Trust that a delay will demand or request greater lucidity. A possible interruption is when one decides to ask for some clarifications way before the speaker is done talking. This is very disappointing as it could make the speaker miss getting to the point they were on their way to. These interferences are possible reasons why the message won't be understood as well as the speaker would have wanted the audience to understand it.

Step 3: Keep an open mind.

Tune in without rationally condemning the things the speaker is trying to let you know. Tune in without making a hasty judgment. Everyone has their own style of communicating, and some may have trouble getting their point across effectively. Be patient and kind. Try to understand that the speaker is using language to share their sentiments.

The only way you will understand what the speaker is trying to put across is by keeping your mind open to the ideas of this person. Try not to be a sentence-grabber by hindering and completing someone else's sentences: odds are, you'll land way off-kilter since you'll be following your very own line of reasoning without realizing, where the speaker's musings were making a beeline for.

Tune in and ensure that all the energy physically is present to enable you to collect the information that is being shared. Once you are completely tuned in, the mind will work to remain on the same page with the speaker and hence understand more of the ideas and pictorial images that will form in the mind.

If it gets to the point where you are supposed to tune in and listen carefully, it is advised that you should not use a lot of your energy for trying to figure out the message that is being shared, but rather relax and first understand the message that is being communicated.

Step 4: Don't interrupt by issuing solutions.

Messages such as the following are caused by barriers, they include:

- "I'm a higher priority here."

- "All I need to state is exact or pertinent."

- "I can make my own decisions."

- "I am not responsible for your energy."

- "I know it is a challenge and not a discussion, and I will definitely win it."

The weight is on the listener to ease up and fit in with a more slow or faster speaker as there are different kinds of speakers and different paces.

Always try to get permission in the event that you feel that you need to put in some ideas and at the very moment that the speaker is flowing with his arrangement. Getting consent is vital for effective communication.

Step 5: Wait for the speaker to pause to ask clarifying questions.

When you did not understand a certain part of their point completely, it is wise to request politely for an explanation. You get this chance when the individual sharing the message pauses. At that point, you ask them politely to repeat on the part that you did not understand.

Step 6: Ask questions only to ensure understanding.

For instance, when a partner or colleague is trying to pass some information about a holiday experience that they had. At that very particular moment, when they are busy going into details about the holiday, you interrupt by asking about the mutual friend the two of you have and before knowing the holiday story stops, and the two of you start discussing the times you had together with the mutual friend.

This type of interruptions happens more frequently then we realize. This will cause the narrator to take a different route than they had not planned about, and after that, they have to start all over again with the initial story, or at times, it does not go back. The speaker may resent the fact that you were unwilling to listen and may hesitate to open up again. This is dangerous in both personal and work-related relationships so try and avoid it.

Step 7: Always try fitting into the emotions of the speaker.

Sympathy is the substance of good tuning in; It is seen when a speaker is narrating to you a sad experience that they had to undergo and instantly, you have to pass your sentiments on to let them know that you felt sorry for them about the experience. Try and put yourself into the speaker's shoes. Perhaps there was a time that you experienced a comparable sadness. With some you may want to share your story to further your show of understanding, and others may not want to hear it if they feel you are trying to overshadow their pain.

Step 8: Give regular feedback.

Demonstrate that you understand what is being communicated to you by showing that you are on the same page with the speaker. "You should be excited!" whenever the experience is breathtaking, happy, or victorious. Try pouring your sentiments by giving instant feedback to the speaker or gesture that you are truly tuned in and understand the experiences of the speaker. Nothing is better than feeling that you are sharing a moment with another.

Step 9: Pay attention to what *isn't* said.

When in a close-up conversation with an individual, it is easy for one to get the difference of happiness and sadness as portrayed in the stories or conversation that both of you are in. It is the non-verbal cues that cannot be passed on with words from the speaker. Perhaps there are things that the speaker would like you to know but cannot convey in words.

Other Aspects That Can Affect Communication

Humor- Regardless of whether you are talking at a workforce gathering, course, or meeting, utilizing humor can help convey data all the more viably to your crowd. Silliness makes your group of spectators feel loose and agreeable.

Cleverness is a helpful instrument to keep their consideration. In the event that you see the crowd with spacey eyes, have a go at tossing out a little surprising funniness and watch their responses. Locate a shared factor with those tuning in to you; simply demonstrate your common and human side, and they will listen more to what you need to say.

Humor can likewise help you approach delicate subjects without making your audience members awkward. Watch your words and express things cautiously. Understand that you can deal with delicate issues with great taste. Be amazingly cautious with silliness when managing touchy issues to abstain from upsetting your audience members. The last thing you want is to be a person that looks to be insulting and arrogant.

On the off chance that you are addressing a not really benevolent gathering, silliness can defuse the pressure and make them less unfriendly towards you and your message. Trust me, you can successfully utilize humor in the event that you end up before a gathering of individuals who have the same dislike and aversions at. Give us a chance to be sensible about this. There will be cases when your group of spectators do not enjoy this type of humor and also occasions when individuals demonstrate their abhorrence for your doled out subject.

When they go into a classroom, they take with them some assumptions about you and the point. These ideas can influence their responses. Your job as a speaker is to get through these confused ideas and win them over to your side. Silliness is one powerful device to separate those hindrances and opposition. It is hard for your group of spectators to differ when they are chuckling and having a fabulous time. Turn it so they will understand that you are entirely on their side and not against them.

Humor on Complicated Topics

Humor can likewise enable you to handle a muddled subject. The more complicated your message, the more you need a diversion to help present the point and make the group of spectators increasingly responsive and open. Diversion establishes the pace for your discussion. It loosens up the group of spectators. A casual setting makes learning fun and more straightforward. It helps if you can rearrange what you need to state and make it increasingly understandable to your group of spectators.

Recognize that the point is entangled and guarantee them that you will put forth a valiant effort to make it as basic and amusing to learn as possible. You need to relate to your crowd, and diversion is the best approach to do only that. It is simpler for them to associate with you on the off chance that they can see you are human like them. Amusingness makes you increasingly agreeable.

So, you proceed with your discussion, and eventually, you understand that your message isn't being comprehended by your group of spectators for reasons unknown. It might be that the room isn't happy, or the group is too enormous and unmanageable. It is difficult to formulate a plan for communication when you have a large and diverse bunch. It is conceivable that the individuals in the group of spectators can't give you their 100% consideration, for they are concerned because the organization is amidst cutting the spending limit and benefits that are so important to their livelihood.

It is additionally conceivable that they are wary in light of the fact that the supervisor is with them or basically on the grounds that they displayed extraordinary aversion and lack of engagement in your point. Break the ice by utilizing proper amusingness.

Guarantee your crowd that you are working for a similar reason, for example, the success of the association. Remind your group of spectators that they ought not to kill the messenger and that you are one of them. In the event that you are a part of the top administration whose duty is to investigate innovative methods for constraining advantages, you may need to figure out how to be amusing rapidly!

Try not to be too cocky about a theme, particularly on the off chance that it is a delicate one, or it includes the lives of individuals. In this circumstance, you can utilize amusingness to help the mind-set and make them open to what you need to state. A clever response to an angry question is fine, you still need to assert your control over the crowd.

When you are attempting to sell a thought, item, or administration to a gathering, humor is progressively significant. On the off chance that you make them snicker, they are bound to tune in to what you need to state. Amusingness can make a few messages simpler to acknowledge.

Open your discourse with accounts or clever individual stories. The idea is to wind up clever and not appear to be a proud and smarty-pants individual. This will most likely be a mood killer for individuals, and it will be exceptionally hard for you to sell whatever you are selling after that.

Before you start adding jokes to your talks, consider cautiously who will be your group of spectators. Jokes and clever stories ought to be proper to your audience members and to the event itself.

Would you like to prevail upon them and make them progressively responsive to your message? Include the group of spectators in your funniness. I don't mean ridicule them or make an individual from your group of spectators the object of jokes. Customize your cleverness to accommodate your group of spectators and the message you are attempting to hand-off. Put yourself in their shoes and remember what their day to day work life might involve. Relatable humor is the best for these moments.

Make them a piece of the message. Take exercise from the best funnies. Include your audience members and cause them to relate and comprehend what you are stating. Noel Coward once stated, "Mind should be a great treat, similar to caviar. Never spread it about like preserves."

Treating People Equally

Great communication is a significant piece of everything being equal and is a basic piece of any solid organization. All connections have good and bad times; a solid conversation style can make it simpler to manage and create a more strong and beneficial association. We frequently hear how significant communication is, yet not what it is and how we can utilize great communication in our connections. Discussing other individuals behind their backs is not encouraged as it creates a harsh environment; hence, it is well when each is treated equally as it will enhance respect and trust among individuals. On the occasion that there is an issue of concern, it is best that it is settled calmly.

In a relationship for example: converse with one another. No matter how strong and well the relationship is with other individuals, no one can tell what the other is thinking. We have to impart unmistakably to stay away from assumptions that may cause hate and disarray, among others.

In a relationship set up, both the involved have different styles and needs that should be taken to account. Couples should come up with the best idea to assist when in disagreement and when one partner feels as if they are not being treated equally. Solid communication requires effort from both parties, and that will make it easy to hold a conversation.

When addressing individuals, one should be clear in order to ensure that the message is understood.

When you converse with your accomplice, attempt to:

- Put aside time to talk without a break from other individuals or interruptions like telephones, PCs, or TV.

- Consider what you need to state.

- Be clear about what you need to convey.

- Make your message unmistakable, with the goal that your accomplice hears it precisely and comprehends what you mean.

- Talk about what's going on and how it influences you.

- Talk about what you need and feel – use 'I' proclamations, for example, 'I need,' and 'I feel.'

- Acknowledge obligation regarding your very own emotions.

- Tune in to your accomplice. Set aside your very own contemplations until further notice and attempt to comprehend their goals, sentiments, needs, and needs (this is called compassion).

- Share positive sentiments with your accomplice, for example, what you acknowledge and respect about them, and that they are so critical to you.

- Know about your manner of speaking.

- Arrange and know that constant correction is not needed at all times. Assume issues that are not of importance and significance or find a third party to address it and help find a solution.

Attempt to Resolve Conflict

Conflict, together with the unavoidable truth, are primarily of a hierarchical life. This develops much when worry creeps in, for example, when there are new changes and no clear instruction on how to cope up with it or at times when individuals are getting the feeling of constraining and lack of enough time.

Nonetheless, conflict can be brought by external factors that have nothing to do with the typical set-up.

A conflict that is handled in a manner that brings pressure and uncomfortable relations is bad for an individual's well-being. Cardiovascular failures and high blood pressure can be caused by handling conflicts in an unhealthy manner, causing the body to react and produce hormones that will mess with its normal operations.

Positive and valuable conflict resolution processes that do not involve pressure on the well-being of an individual are significant methods that can be used to improve the relationship with others.

This, in a deeper sense, means:

• It's wise to understand that conflicts and situations that contradict mutual understanding are present normally.

• The interrelation of one another dictates that individuals should rely on one another in different circumstances. This doesn't mean that their efforts and energy have to be equal but just the motivation and understanding that they could achieve more by working together.

• The individuals have to acknowledge that the objectives set are bigger than their disagreements.

• They are going after assets; hence making them not to gain the big objective.

Conflict can be ruinous, driving individuals to create negative affections for one another and spend vitality on the strife that could be better spent somewhere else. It can likewise develop contrasts, and lead gatherings to spellbind into either/or positions.

Be that as it may, well-overseen conflict can likewise be productive, clearing 'the air,' discharging feeling and stress, and settling strain, particularly if those included use it as a chance to build comprehension and discover a route forward together out of the contention circumstance.

Smile and Hold on to a Positive Attitude

No particular individual who would like to associate themselves with other hopeless individuals. Therefore, it is wise that everyone tries to live together in harmony and maintain good relationships with friends and people from the same area. Be positive at all times and be keen to live, and hopeful that things will soon work out even when they seem to not be going so well. Once you are noticed to be the disturbing one, it is then when everyone will do their best to avoid you at all costs.

People gravitate towards positive people and at the same time being positive can make a bad situation better. Attitude is everything. It is advisable that you should not be quick to make moves whenever something is not going according to plan. By chance, if you have to make a move or try to translate the situation, try to stay positive about the whole situation by avoiding stressful conclusions.

Try to Minimize Stress

Some situations are, by their temperament, distressing. Stress is a possible factor to hinder good communication, and all individuals should try their best to avoid it and stay cool.

Stress can also be detrimental to your physical and mental health. There is no mistake that the effects of stress can cause many physical ailments, from something as simple as a headache to heart attack and disease. Remove as much stress as you can so you don't end up in an even more stressful situation.

There are a couple of ways you can work to minimize stress. For example:

Taking care of yourself - Individuals are better ready to adapt to pressure when their bodies are solid.

This is halfway on the grounds that when you are fit and well, you can basically adapt to additional, and incompletely on the grounds that weakness is in itself a significant wellspring of stress.

There are three primary territories to see: diet, exercise, and rest.

- Setting aside a few minutes for physical exercise in your standard day will improve muscle control, make you feel more advantageous and increment confidence. You may feel that you don't have time. However, the advantages will more than reimburse the 30 minutes or so away from your plan for the day.

- Attempt to improve your eating regimen and maintain a strategic distance from stimulants; however much as could be expected. Abundance caffeine or nicotine can make people feel on edge or nervous. It very well may entice to go to lousy nourishment to spare time; however, it won't help you in the long haul. Setting aside some effort to prepare a feast, regardless of whether it is just something straightforward, is useful in mitigating pressure since it makes you feel that you are taking care of yourself.

- You additionally need to guarantee that you get enough rest. Try not to attempt to work or do things until you wish to fall into bed.

Rather, take thirty minutes or so before you hit the sack to loosen up a bit. Doing some physical exercise can likewise assist you with sleeping better since it implies your body is drained and your mind is clear.

Think positively - Your brain is a groundbreaking thing. It can drag you down, and it can likewise develop you.

When we are focused on, it is enticing to concentrate on everything that is difficult, or that is turning out badly in our lives. Nonetheless, thinking all the more decidedly—for instance, by seeing what has gone well that day or week, or even over a more extended period—can effectively affect your disposition.

It is worth intentionally abstaining from dwelling on any disappointments and ensuring that you compensate yourself for your victories. You have to acknowledge that everybody has restraints and can't prevail at everything and revel in what you have accomplished.

Seek support from others - Try not to feel that you need to adapt to your issues alone. Requesting help is frequently hard, yet it is an awesome initial move towards dealing with your pressure better.

Having somebody to share your issues can incredibly 'off burden' the pressure. You may think that it's helpful to converse with a companion or work associate. You can likewise converse with your line administrator or manager on the off chance that you are encountering worry in the working environment.

Introduction to Emotional Intelligence

The art of knowing how to deal with your self-emotions as well as for those that are around is known as Emotional intelligence or EI. It is wise to get to know the different feelings that we have, get to understand them, and as well acknowledge that our inner feelings can greatly influence us in what we do for ourselves as well as others.

Having enthusiastic insight is fundamental for progress in every individual. Everything considered, which individual is more likely to progress among the following – a boss who talks arrogantly to their employees anytime they are under pressure or a boss who remains calm and collected, no matter the circumstances that are present.

Professor Daniel Goleman, an American author who was well-skilled to understand emotional intelligence wrote the following:

"**Self-awareness** is vital for an individual to know and understand their feelings and the outcome of the feelings, and understand that they can impact the people around you negatively or positively. Being in charge of a gathering prompts that one has to understand their feelings so as not to pass them down to the others, by behaving good and being mindful of the outcomes of your actions."

How does an individual work to manage and improve their emotional intelligence?

Keep notes, such as journals, that will help your mind have a grasp on your actions. By taking time each day to jot down a few observations about your own behavior, you can impact your general outcome of behavior positively.

Slow down anytime something upsets you. Take time and try to understand why it had to be that way. Always remember that whatever the circumstances that happen, it is your sole decision to choose how to react to it.

Self-regulation by knowing what the personal limits are when indulging in with others by being mindful of what you say and react to their actions. It is a good habit to get into, to know and understand your limits and at the same time, not compromise on what you want to settle for.

As per Goleman, this completely covers individual adaptability and responsibility.

That being said, how might one improve your capacity for self-regulation?

Know your qualities – Having clear lines of the things you want and those that you do not want.

Knowing what are the major qualities that benefit you the most. Put in some energy, paying attention to your "code of morals." This makes it easy for you at any particular moment that you encounter two choices and hence, you will not waste time deliberating on them but go straight and pick what is best for you.

Be responsible – Try and not blame people all the time for things that do not turn out perfect. Always take responsibility for the wrongs that you have done and move on.

Work on being quiet – At any particular time when in disagreement or conflict with anyone, try as much to take time before reacting by thinking through the actions.

Likewise, always jot down the negative things that push you down and work on them to improve yourself. Pouring the feeling on paper and not actually to any individual is vital for personal growth. This assists your personal growth and the relationship between you and the people around you.

Motivation – Self-motivated individuals always work on their objectives and pull all the resources that assist them in achieving it.

Inspiration can be improved by?

Confirm again the reason as to why you are indulging in your responsibility. You will always put first what you hold dear above everything else in situations where you have to choose between two options. Be sure to why you really need to do it. In a situation where you may be confused as to what to pick, you could use the 5 whys strategy to assist you in making a decision.

Ensure that the objections at hand are empowering.

Know your stand – Determine at which particular position you can actually serve better. In a business kind of setup, you can determine if you are the boss or the employee and whether you are easily persuaded or not.

Have confidence and make a great discovery. - Individuals who are motivated have many ideas despite the circumstance. Getting this attitude takes practice and is always justified.

Try to discover one benefit about a circumstance every time you are faced with a test or a disappointment. No matter the magnitude of the circumstance, try to find something positive about it because, in one way or another, you might have dealt with something similar.

Empathy – Being sympathetic might affect an individual's relationship with others. Such individuals are able to place themselves in the shoes of others. These individuals take the initiative in assisting others who are having a hard time to express themselves.

Be sympathetic at that particular moment where you gain trust from the group and let the trust grow.

Ways to improve your sympathy?

Place yourself in another individual's shoes. Not unless you actually experience another person's story, only then will you be able to understand the situation that they are going through. It is not an easy task, but you have to step up to show your sympathy and offer a shoulder to lean on.

Focus on non-verbal communication – By nibbling your lips, folding your arms and moving your feet to and fro while an individual is sharing their experience shows a great amount of non-verbal communication. This shows that you are paying attention to the experience of being narrated. Understanding non-verbal communication requires a great set of skills as it will show you how to react perfectly to a situation as much as distinguishing the truth about the story.

Show reaction to sentiments –For instance in work set up you request a workmate to cover up for you once more, and he agrees but in a faint voice, discuss it with him that you understand his working additional hours and that you need them to extend and work late in order to achieve the objective and target that was set before them. By discussing this with a partner, it shows that you care for them.

Social skills – People who are good at social abilities are considered intelligent and smart communicators. These people are able to change situations that appear sad and rephrase them to suit the group and matters at hand. Individuals who are good at social skills are also able to settle disagreements and clashes in particular groupings or situations. These individuals have an option not to intervene in conflicts and disagreements, but they do not relax, sit back and observe. Instead, they take the initiative and find solutions to the problem.

Ways to build social skills?

Compromise – People with leadership skills understand that at times, things have to be done differently, and not everyone has to be happy about them. Hence they have to compromise in order to get solutions.

Improving your relational abilities– People who understand that not everyone is alike are good at relationship abilities because they handle everyone differently according to their understanding.

Learn to appreciate others – A leader knows how to appreciate his subordinates as he understands the needs of each and every one of them and knows that they worked so hard to get the appreciation.

As a leader, the growth of being effective and passionate will not be instant, as time is a key factor in achieving almost all of the points mentioned and time itself playing a big role in testing your patience. Hence, your subordinates also test your limits.

Chapter 3: Run Effective Meeting.

Set the table.

There are great meetings, and there are awful meetings. Awful gatherings ramble on always, you never appear to arrive at the point, and you leave asking why you were even present. Viable ones leave you invigorated and feeling that you've truly achieved something.

Some gatherings are day-to-day lifestyle. This creates chances for effective meetings and sharing of information as well as skills.

An individual moving the motion of a particular gathering is important. These kinds of gatherings are where ideas of visioning, creating networks, conceptualizing, venture planning, organizational audits, staff meetings, creation of organization visions, as well as putting objectives and activities for the employees on the memos.

The factors that make the gatherings happen to allow for a wide range of communication not limited to the ones mentioned.

Most individuals think that all the success of an organization can be achieved just by holding one or two gatherings while it actually takes a lot of effort both from the administration and the employees. In such meetings, it is advisable to have the motion mover who will be responsible for the time and the plan that was set prior to the gathering, and his responsibility will be to make sure that all points have been discussed in order to achieve the goals.

Only three factors can make a meeting effective.

• First of all, the planning of the meeting needs to be set and arranged in such a manner that the meeting will focus on the most pressing issues to those that do not require so many efforts.

• Oversee (and practice) your gathering presentations cautiously. You need to ensure that your members feel that their gathering has clear reason and effect.

• Keep in mind, to utilize the integrative and plural first individual of 'we' or 'us' and evade the particular 'I' with the goal that you can start to move obligation and possession to the members since they claim the outcomes.

Before your meeting: the plan.

Before you start your gathering presentation, have your room set-up to outwardly show the reason, extension, and deliverable of any workshop. In the event that you can't change over these three core values into 50 words or less (for every), at that point, you are not prepared at this point to dispatch the workshop. Allow us to rehash, on the off chance that you don't have a clue what the deliverable resembles; at that point, you don't have a clue what achievement resembles.

Consider showing the reason, degree, and deliverable paper, alongside a lot of standard procedures proper to your governmental issues and circumstance. The accompanying gathering presentation grouping is normally ideal for a hearty beginning.

A meeting where nobody has done what they vowed to do at the last one is dead from the earliest starting point.

It's a typical enough situation, but it's one that can frequently be maintained a strategic distance from basically by ensuring that sufficient notes are circled instantly after each gathering. That way, with the talk still crisp in individuals' psyches, everybody has an unmistakable token of what they have to do.

Obviously, we're not going to imagine that note composing is an exciting action or an especially energizing part of your vocation. However, unmistakably composed, exhaustive, and sorted out notes can be extremely ground-breaking.

They can have the effect between the individuals who went to the gathering leaving and sitting idle, or really doing what's required so as to push a task ahead. What's more, that progress could be an immediate consequence of your notes!

Plan

Before you plan a gathering, first choose what it is you need the gathering to achieve and who should be there. A gathering is a method for passing on data — one that accommodates a two-way exchange. It tends to be utilized to accumulate contribution to choices or guarantee arrangements in the working environment.

Be that as it may, in case you're giving data and not looking for an exchange, a gathering may not be your most profitable technique for communication. Maybe you could send an email or record a brisk sound or video message? Everything begins with what you need to achieve.

Planning the meeting area.

The plan gives the centering structure to the gathering, places assignments in an intelligent request and time allotment, and offers a blueprint for composing the rundown report at the meeting's decision.

In the hands of a gifted facilitator, a plan ought to be viewed as a rule, not a law. Adaptability is basic to guarantee that points are settled or errands achieved in an ideal way. Facilitators ought to envision which things could be delayed and be set up to table them until an increasingly fitting time.

The procedure plan has the extra data the facilitator and meeting pioneers need to guarantee that the gathering runs easily. Assembling the nitty-gritty procedure motivation enables the gathering heads to thoroughly consider the subtleties of the whole session.

Normal room arrangement alternatives incorporate the following;

Meeting Styles - Members are situated on four sides of a table. This style is frequently utilized for little board gatherings or comparable gatherings.

Square - On this particular arrangement, tables are arranged equally insides such as that of a square hence leaving a gap in the middle. This type of sitting arrangement is important where a big number of people are expected, and they need to brainstorm.

U-Shape - This particular arrangement looks like the letter U of the alphabetical order. This is more effective at gatherings that have a central source of information, and hence, they need to be focused on one side, which in this case is the open side.

Theater Style - Columns of seats are set by one another, confronting the front of the room. A speaker or moderator is at the front of the room. This style amplifies the accessible seating and functions admirably when the group of spectators needs to take negligible notes, and when member collaboration will be negligible.

Study hall Style - Lines of tables face the front of the stay with two to four seats at each. This arrangement is proper when there is an introduction at the front of the room, and members are relied upon to take notes.

Round Tables - Eight to ten seats are organized around little round tables. This style can be utilized for little breakout gatherings. Members can banter with one another effectively.

Figure out What You Want to Accomplish

A gathering ought to have a reason; for example, venture refreshes exercise educated, or client criticism. On the off chance that you can't think about a reason, there might be no compelling reason to meet. "Week by week or month to month" organization gatherings, for instance, fill no need except if you know ahead of time what you need to escape each gathering occasion.

Before you plan a gathering, ask yourself: why you have to meet? Questions that can enable you to decide if a gathering is the best utilization of your or your participants' time are:

- Is there data I have to impart to participants that is mind-boggling to such an extent that they'll have the option to pose inquiries about it?

- Are there choices on which I need participants to give criticism?

- Are there worries that I should be certain everybody hears and sees so they can help fix them?

- Is there recognition that I need to partake before the group to propel others to perform at a more significant level?

- Are there task refreshes that colleagues need to think about, so they realize what to do straightaway?

- Does the group have data or bits of knowledge that I or others have to think about?

- Are there preparing or wellbeing methods that should be audited, refreshed, or comprehended?

Set and Document an Agenda

The agenda gives the centering system to the gathering, places assignments in a legitimate request and time allotment, and offers a framework for composing the outline report at the meeting's decision.

There are regularly two renditions of an agenda. The membership plan is the brief adaptation members get before a gathering. At the very least, the member plan incorporates the gathering title, area, start and end times, goals, dialog points, also, data about how and when participants will take part. The agenda is a reasonable and streamlined variant of the itemized procedure motivation.

To help plan for your gathering, and affirm that a gathering is the best approach, build up motivation. The motivation will diagram what you need to achieve, how much time you figure it will take, and who will be the best individual to show every point or potentially encourage criticism on it.

We've given a basic gathering motivation layout above, and a model beneath to enable you to thoroughly consider your subjects. This motivation layout can be utilized to control you in arranging your gathering and thoroughly considering who needs to visit.

A meeting has to have a leader who will be responsible for the time the meeting is running. Successful meetings are fascinating, high-vitality occasions where colleagues cooperate to settle on choices or take care of issues. Shockingly, an excessive number of the gatherings we go to appear to be the exact inverse. The most noticeably awful gatherings carry time to a slither leaving everybody rationally and genuinely depleted and quite bit baffled. The thing that matters is how the gatherings are arranged and run.

The best leader comprehends the significance of these occasions, and they comprehend that creating an incredible gathering requires arranging and intentional exertion. The following are hints to enable you to exploit this significant joint effort time with your group. Tips on the best way to fortify your meeting as a leader are as follows:

Have a Positive Attitude about Meetings.

It is the absolute most significant thing a director can do as a pioneer to improve group gatherings. It's amazing what a number of chiefs are glad to announce their abhorrence of gatherings; however, to meet huge results, solve issues, decide, illuminate, move, team up, and inspire, directors need to work with individuals.

That is actually organizing a meeting either personally or by phone, where all the individuals have to be present. Overseeing isn't tied in with sitting in the workplace with the entryway shut, sending messages. As a pioneer, take a stab at taking a gander at gatherings as the sign of administration. It's authority showtime, not something to fear like an outing to the dental specialist.

Keep in mind that You Own the Meeting.

Try not to assign the motivation intending to a clerical specialist or another colleague. As the pioneer, it's your gathering to plan and run. To place yourself in the correct outlook, ask, and answer the accompanying inquiry: "After this gathering, what will I need individuals to have learned, accomplished, or fathomed?"

Request Input on the Agenda.

In spite of the fact that it's the director's essential obligation to build up the motivation, colleagues can be welcome to contribute plan things. Convey a call for thoughts a couple of days before the gathering.

Allow the "blank area" for Spontaneous Creativity and Engagement.

Try not to pack such a large number of things on the plan that you battle to finish it. Rather, leave some room toward the end for unconstrained talk. In the event that the gathering closes early, at that point, let everybody go early. Everybody acknowledges discovered time too.

Use Team Meetings to Collaborate.

Rather than simply sharing data, take a stab at taking care of an issue or working with the gathering on landing at a choice. Indeed, it's difficult and can be chaotic, yet that is the place we get the most incentive from gatherings.

Lighten Up.

Being the pioneer of a gathering isn't tied in with parading authority or mishandling power. Berating somebody for being late before the group is a case of doing this. Keep a comical inclination and your quietude.

Be a Role Model Leader.

Meetings are not a platform for you to defend yourself by discrediting others with the intention to make yourself look much better than others. Try and make the meeting a general talk and, more especially, on the issues that relate to every person that is present in the meeting. Avoid the use of bad jokes, mockery and bad jokes as this is what distinguishes you from being a good leader and it makes the bond between everyone much stronger. Be the role model every member of the organization looks up to.

Choose Who Needs to Be There.

Numerous workers severely dislike going to gatherings, on the grounds that, to be honest, they're exhausting if the substance isn't applicable to the members. Along these lines, just welcome to your gathering the individuals whose info or updates you need. On the off chance that your gathering is intended to design a task, welcome the individuals who have a stake in it. In the event that the gathering is to get a choice, just welcome those whose feelings will be considered.

That may imply that you have more, however littler, gatherings. Rather than requiring a gigantic unforeseen of representatives to go to a huge group meeting, think about whether just a little piece of the motivation relates to them. It is in this way, lead a shorter gathering on simply that subject, with just the people whose info or purchase is required on that point.

Choose Format, Time, and Location.

Notwithstanding making sense of who to visit, and what you're attempting to achieve with your gathering, you'll need to pick a configuration for the gathering. For instance, in the event that you need a brisk choice that includes various individuals, a short phone meeting (telephone call) may get the job done. Inquiries regarding your gathering organization may include:

- Do we have to meet face to face, up close, and personal?

- Should the gathering be in private (out of earshot of others)?

- Would we be able to do the gathering through phone meetings? (Or on the other hand, include a telephone line so remote/voyaging members can visit?)

- Would a gathering led by means of video meeting better suit our participants?

In case you're talking about delicate data or an issue that is effectively misjudged, one on one gatherings are best as they enable the gathering participants to pose inquiries and read non-verbal communication, just as hear reactions.

A few gatherings, for example, those that spread monetary data or worker changes like cutbacks, may be held in a private region or offsite to keep others from hearing secret data.

In the event that your group is remote, the best configuration might be a video meeting. That decreases travel and can get everybody in the equivalent "room" a lot quicker. Your gathering arrangement can be added to your motivation layout with the goal that everybody on the welcome rundown knows about how you intend to meet.

Welcome Attendees

Before holding the meeting it is polite to chat while you wait for the meeting to begin. It would be better to discuss things unrelated to the meeting, such as weather, family or weekend plans. Once everyone arrives, you should formally welcome everyone to the meeting and thank the participants for coming.

If the meeting is a small group, it is probably not necessary to take the participation out loud. You will know everyone personally and can indicate who is present and who is absent. In a larger meeting, you may need to send an attendance sheet or call names. If an important figure is absent, you may need to apologize for his absence and offer a brief explanation.

During Your Meeting: Running the Meeting.

How you start and end your gathering are two factors that will improve your gathering adequacy. As people, we like to be social and make up for lost time with what's new with our companions. Gatherings give a scene to that. In any case, an excessive amount of socialization can be troublesome to your gathering motivation.

In the event that your participants don't generally get the chance to see each other, consider requesting that they join a couple of minutes early, with the goal that your genuine gathering can begin on schedule.

Overseeing Time.

Time points of confinement are a basic piece of well-run gatherings. Despite the fact that time cutoff points can make tension, most members will value beginning and finishing on time more than they will hate the weight of time limits.

The initial step is to guide out time constraints for every movement on the plan. Make sure every movement is given a particular measure of time that is satisfactory to address the issue. Practice exercises before the gathering to test the time presumptions, and, utilizing this data, build up time limits for speakers, exchange, and less organized exercises. Consider naming a timekeeper and giving that individual power to stop individuals, with sufficient notice (e.g., a "two-minute sign" or other signal), when their time is up. Having a noticeable check in the room is additionally useful.

Here once more, the need to be adaptable is foremost. The facilitator or meeting pioneer must realize what motivation things can be put off to another gathering, chose rapidly, or designated to a member or subcommittee to choose. Facilitators must be prepared to change the motivation during the gathering, as required, with a definitive objective of achieving meeting targets while giving everybody a chance to leave on schedule.

Welcome and Greet Attendees.

Some gathering organizers like to begin their gatherings with a culture or group building action to exploit the eye to eye time that participants have together. They consider group building or culture-building some portion of their gathering reason.

Yet, regardless of whether you don't have a relationship expanding at the forefront of your thoughts, it's useful to welcome your participants as they show up (no uniquely in contrast to you would welcome clients strolling in your entryway). Tell them what you want to achieve. For instance, you could state, "I'm happy you're here. We'll begin in five minutes. I'm anticipating every one of us being in agreement after this gathering." This helps center your participants' consideration around for what reason they're there.

Review the Agenda and Get Feedback.

While it feels formal, a motivation audit truly sets the stage and can keep your gathering on track. For instance, if your gathering is on security transforms, you may cover the consequences of an ongoing wellbeing review, and need to execute three suggested changes. At that point, maybe you'll take inquiries toward the end. This gives participants a core interest. It's additionally not an awful way to deal with giving them a time period as well, for example, "we want to be done before early afternoon."

Before you dispatch into your subjects, inquire as to whether there's anything identified with the theme that they'd like to ensure you spread. For instance, maybe one participant has an inquiry on how they should share wellbeing concerns, or another needs to realize where to discover the MSDS.

On the off chance that you like the recommendation, you can add it to your motivation. If not, you can record it and recommend it's a discussion you'll plan later or one-on-one. In either case, you've made participants feel like they're a piece of the gathering, not latent onlookers.

Work Through Your Agenda Items.

Work through every motivation thing. You could kick each off, spread the subject, request criticism, and move to the following thing. Or then again, you could pose that all inquiries be held until the end. A best practice is to draw in your participants during the gathering to avert, making your gathering a monolog.

To do that, have various participants partake in showing the data, discourse theme, or choice criteria. That way, you can encourage the gathering, and your participants have a stake in the gathering and its results.

Park Items That Don't Belong in the Meeting

It will happen that somebody will raise a subject or worry that is just extraneously identified with the gathering point, or not in the slightest degree related. In the event that you need your participants to remain connected with, your most solid option is to stop those thoughts on a parking area and offer to catch up later.

Record Next Steps.

A major misstep that entrepreneurs and people make when leading gatherings isn't catching the following stages. On the off chance that you've settled on a choice at a gathering, for example, to change a technique or to finish a venture, that choice should be recorded and followed up. Something else, the words drift into the air until the following gathering, when somebody will, in the long run, say, "Whatever happened to that?"

As it were, somebody needs to claim the follow-up for each activity thing, choice, or subsequent stage.

You can utilize the subsequent stages area of our layout above to record results, choices, and subsequent meet-ups. Allot a proprietor to each. It is anything but a poorly conceived notion to give a subsequent date, so every understanding made is finished inside a particular time allotment.

After your meeting: Recap & follow up.

On the off chance that it's significant enough to have a gathering on a theme, it's significant enough to catch up with it. You can do this by sending a speedy email to help participants to remember what they've consented to. Or on the other hand, you can timetable venture assignments to be certain that subsequent stages are taken and finished.

With the expectation of complimentary undertaking the board programming that can be utilized to follow due dates and expectations in any industry, consider utilizing keen scrutiny of the situation. It enables you to design your exercises and work process to meet your definite business needs.

You can likewise archive the subsequent assignments directly on our layout. Things to follow-up on might include:

- Updates about due dates for the individuals who have acknowledged explicit undertakings

- Follow-up on activity things, for example, data you've vowed to give

- Changes to methodology or documentation that should be made

- Criticism on the most proficient method to improve gatherings going ahead

On the off chance that you need to decide if your gathering was important, you should seriously mull over sending an input study, posing inquiries like: What did you find generally significant? How might we improve our next gathering?

Free review instruments like Survey Monkey are one of a few free business applications that you may discover accommodating for your private venture.

Chapter 4: Effective Written Communication

Write it down

Written communication is the kind of communication that incorporates the use of words. Communication is a vital element for bringing understanding between any two individuals or gatherings. Writing of letters and messages on paper is in the current world losing popularity as most people are switching to the use of data exchange by use of applications and sites. As much as this is happening, written communication is the most widely used form of communication.

In a business set up, written communication is the formal and official type of communication as the bosses and managers use it to pass on messages and instructions to the employees, and the employees do the same in return as a form of feedback. In as much as we still write, the era of data exchange has changed a few ways on how written communication was done in the earlier years.

There is a need to make the use of written communication a thing again as the passion and motivation to do it is slowly dying with the coming of the data exchange era. Businesses and other firms should make the use of written communication, the official way of communication even with the external partners and clients, as this also creates a backup of the history of the parties involved.

That being said, "the words we write and share are a true definition of us and our businesses. We should make sure that the deep message sent in our e-mails says good things about the organization." clarified Janis Fisher Chan, author of "E-Mail: A Write It Well Guide - How to Write and Manage E-Mail in the Workplace". Written communication objective is to pass information the way it is while remaining relevant and precise about it to make the other reader understand it easily. Individuals go through official written communication so as to get direct instructions and ideas from the responsible writers.

Official written communication carries with them a sense of command and urgency, unlike friendly written communications that can be ignored. The format to which a written directive is put can tell the seriousness of the writer as well as the urgency of the message being conveyed. Clear, direct and polite tone in a written communication medium is the best format and way to write the message.

Murphy and Herbert W. Hildebrandt, the authors of "Effective Business Communications", wrote that great communication should be clear, readable, kind, concrete, right, and considerate of the reader. This actually means that effective written communications should: provide answers to essential inquiries like what, when, who and whys; be short and to the point; reply to the specific inquiries; make use of numbers and words in a dynamic manner; provide illustrations where possible; be polite and precise.

Written Communication advantages include:

- Written communication sets down clear and precise instructions in an association that helps it run effectively.

- It helps in record keeping as copies of the written communication are available for perusal at any time.

- It facilitates by giving direct instructions of duties and objectives.

- Written communication gives precise and direct guidelines.

- Well jotted written communication plays as a factor in elevating the picture of an organization.

- It provides references for future use.

- Legitimate barriers are within this communication as records are available.

Disadvantages of Written Communication include:

- Written communications are much more expensive as they incorporate the use of resources such as papers, pens, and ink. They also need storage places that require funds to make available.

- This kind of communication does not support instant reactions, especially in a situation where the sender and receiver are far from each other. Written communication demands prompt actions, and hence, a lot of energy is consumed doing that.

- For efficient written communication, an individual with good knowledge of the language, as well as the dialects, is needed to make it a successful mode of communication.

- Bulky desk work and message weight is included.

Writing Effective Emails.

Emails are an effective way of communication, but to some individuals, it is a challenge. When an individual does not understand the message that is being communicated to them, then miscommunication is a possibility. Email writing is used in a number of circumstances, including the writing to get an inquiry, job search, and applications, requesting assistance or guidelines in business setup, and communicating reports to bosses as well as workmates sharing data.

When writing emails, one has to be keen to direct the message to the people to whom it concerns so as to achieve effectiveness as they will understand the data quickly.

Email choice of communication is best applicable where:

- You are passing a message to persons that you do not meet personally on a regular basis, or they are not reachable by other means of communication.

- Whenever there is a physical communication barrier, emails are more significant and are a way to communicate with one another.

- The message that is intended to be sent across does not have a limited time frame, and hence, the reply could be expected in the coming days as well and weeks.

- For other specific emails, it is advisable that instructions on when and how to reply to them should be indicated for the reader to understand and follow the instruction.

- There is a need or responsibility to share with someone some piece of evidence electronically where physical means are not achievable.

- Written emails are useful when there in multiple targeted recipients for the message, and hence, you can send a single email to a number of recipients.

It is vital to hold copies of the records of the communication you have had with other individuals for future reference that is vital in cases of proof of buying of items, copies for an audit of the organization. This is only possible when you use the email as a communication means.

Barriers in Email as a form of communication.

Too much information that at times confuses the reader while it would be easier to hold a one on one conversation with the recipient in order for them to understand it quickly and save time. By sending an email, the response time is not guaranteed to be short.

In the event that two individuals are communicating through email and the contents of the emails are confidential, the chances are that the emails are being read by a third party in some particular area, and it is not known to the two original people. Emails are considered not to be safe and private as other individuals can get access to communication.

Emails that are not written in a manner that is easy for the reader to understand could hinder the response time that is needed for the particular message, and hence, it is discouraged to use email if the sender needs prompt reaction on the details.

Who is your crowd?

Individuals have various conclusions on what email ought to resemble, so it is constantly useful to know about the desires for your crowd. For instance, a few people view email as a fast and casual type of communication—an approach to state "hi" or to pose a brisk inquiry. Be that as it may, others view email as essentially an increasingly advantageous approach to transmit a proper letter. Some individuals will consider friendly emails to be impolite and non-ethical.

When sending the email, make sure that it is sent to the people whom the information is supposed to reach and the one who will find it relevant. Avoid sending emails to random people.

You need to consider the type of relationship that you hold with the people that you are sending the email to by knowing how often they check their emails. This is a vital factor to consider before pressing the Send button.

When writing an email, make sure to draft it in a manner that when the reader takes a look at the arrangement and design that the message has been sent because the email will speak volumes to who the sender really is like in terms of fluency of language as well as the skill to communicate.

Important components of an effective email:

Titles

When writing an email, be sure to give some kind of summary at the title of the email that gives a hint of what the email body really is expounding on. This will help the reader to tune their minds to what type of information they are about to read. When the reader sees the titles of the emails, they are able to strategize on the way to reply to them by order of the most important and urgent emails to the rest that is not of urgency.

Greetings and Sign-offs

Effective emails have the greetings and sign-off sections where the individual writing it will salute and sign out on the reader. This creates some sort of environment between the sender and receiver before they start writing on the matter at hand. In the event that you are not familiar with the individual that you are sending the email to, it is wise to use simple and polite salutations that are general and do not limit them to being male or female. Some of these general and polite salutations and sign-offs include:

- *"Dear sir/madam"*

- *"Kind regards"*

- *"Yours sincerely"*

- *"Yours truly"*

On the account that you have an idea of whom you are sending the email to, it is wise that you salute them by their official names or the official occupation titles in order to show respect. Examples of the same include:

- *Dear doctor Mark,*

- *Hi, Mrs. Mekka,*

- *Hello there, John,*

In the event that you have no idea of who you are addressing to be it an individual or a representative to a group of people. It could as well be that the email is addressed to anyone who will come across it in a particular organization. Here are some ideas on how to salute in search situations:

- *To whomever, it may concern,*

- *Dear members of the golf club,*

- *Hi, everybody,*

Your end is critical on the grounds that it tells the peruser who is reaching them. Continuously close down with your name toward the finish of your message. In the event that you don't have a clue about the peruser well, you may likewise consider including your title and the association you have a place with; for instance:

- *Andrew Golden,*

- *Senior pastor,*

- *Baptist church,*

Or:

- *Joseph Sutherland*

- *Professor University of Colorado,*

For your end, something brief however inviting, or maybe simply your name, will accomplish for generally communication:

- *Many thanks to you,*

- *All the best,*

- *Kind regards,*

For a formal message, for example, an employment form, make use of the sign off to show honesty and hope that you may find in a business letter:

- *Sincerely,*

- *Genuinely,*

Cc: (Carbon Copy) and Bcc: (Blind Carbon Copy)

Writing an email and being able to send the same to a number of recipients is a common method of communication. This is possible when you need to share the same message to different people who are necessarily in the same location. This helps to minimize work in volumes where an individual, for instance, a supervisor, needs to send emails to all the employees addressing the same issue in an organization.

Understand that when you CC people on an email, the people in the To: field and in the CC: field will all receive the same message. They'll also be able to read the email address of other recipients.

Blind Carbon Copy of information (Bcc:) is very helpful at the moment that the sender does not want the recipients to get information of the other recipients of the same chain of email. The only receiver that is visible to all the others is the one in the To: field alone. Those at the Bcc: segment is not visible to the others but only the sender is able to see them.

Consider that Bcc: doesn't work like CC: when it comes to email replies. For example, if you send an email to Mike and BCC: to Sarah, Sarah will receive the original email you send. However, if Mike replies, Sarah won't get a copy of Mike's reply. Mike's email program can't see that Sarah ever received the original message, so it doesn't send her a copy of the reply.

Effectively writing the e-mail.

Think through the message before writing it down. For a start, you need to establish the reason as to why you are writing and what kind of reply do you wait to get from the other end. While doing that, plan as to whom the recipients of the message will be and how well to package the message so that they would understand it and promptly reply to it. This way the message will be easy to understand and save time. Note down a few points that you have to make sure they appear in the message as they are the core reason as to why you are writing.

The tone as to which you write the message is vital. Word in the emails does not carry with them tones and voice expressions, so this can cause a reader to misread the general tone of the email body. Jokes are hardly put down in emails as there is a high possibility for them to be misread and hence might cause anger to the reader. At the same time, as discussed before, it is wise that you pick the best way to salute the reader of the messages as this creates a nice environment to start with.

Make sure that you are clear and straight to the point when writing the email. Miscommunication is possible in an event where the message being sent is not complete, hazy, complicated, and direct. The following are tips on how to make sure that the message you write is understood clearly:

- Be quick to bring to the reader's attention your motivation as to why you are writing at the earliest part of the email body.

- For inquiry purposes, be quick to refer to the issues that you are inquiring about, for instance, payment of dividends and salaries. This is best done by referencing the exact particular email that should be useful in the inquiry.

- Create a new chain of emails in the event where there is a long chain of emails that might confuse the reader.

Before the conclusion of the message, you should be sure to mention the main points of the email. In an event you are proposing a particular reply that you expect, do that in a very polite manner leaving it open as it is the choice of the receiver to do that. At the end of the email, for instance, in a business set up, mention that you are looking forward to the communication as it will be of assistance to you " or "We should plan to meet and talk about this on Wednesday").

Make use of the void areas of the email to take time and expound on issues that matter. Expound the issues to the reader so that they should not get a hard time understanding the message that you are putting through. It is vital to give examples of cases where data is vital in the email reply. Do not forget to date the email as it is good for future reference.

Always proofread the email before sending it. This guarantees that you did mention every issue that you had planned to. It also checks for language and grammar mistakes that should be avoided. Check for punctuation mistakes by the use of applications that help in making writing effective. Before sending the email, make sure to go through it once more so as to confirm that the message will be understood easily by the reader.

How to improve written communication.

Writing is the most significant mode of communication that every employee, boss, and student must be good at. Researchers also utilize writing to put down their findings. Writing compensates for the moments when an individual is not fluent enough to communicate by means of speech.

Spelling, punctuation, and word arrangements errors are evidently clear in written communication. Being fluent in writing does not guarantee the ability to possess the information or even poor writing skill. In a school set up, written communication can enable a teacher to rate the proficiency abilities of the students. In a work setting, people may rate your professionalism by the way you articulate issues in an organization by the way you send data to your employees.

They are likewise prone to expect your verbally expressed capacity in English is very low. However, this could conceivably be the situation. That is the reason it is critical to improving composing abilities in English before they keep you from arriving at your maximum capacity at school or in the working environment.

Luckily, the more regularly you compose, the simpler it will be to get to the English you are searching for and convey what needs be precisely and easily. Scientists realize that on the off chance that you are a solid author in your first language, odds are you will likewise be a solid essayist in English.

That is on the grounds that system use moves. Be that as it may, you can generally figure out how to be progressively key as an essayist and improve your abilities by pursuing a class.

An arrangement course, even one went for local speakers, will enable you to improve the manner in which you respond to various writings, sort out your thoughts and unite jargon, language, and tone to upgrade your composition. Spelling and familiarity, with regards to the real procedure of putting words on paper, can be improved by taking an online course.

Remember that you can't figure out how to compose the medium-term. It's a procedure, and the more you compose and get criticism on your composed work, the more grounded you will turn into.

How writing works - Start with a transposition of your thoughts into written language, trying to make the reader follow your reasoning. Subsequently, move on to the review phase to identify the most exact and convincing formulation that makes thoughts clear and concise. In the end, make sure there are no sentence structures, spelling, or other errors in text organization that may distract the reader from what you are saying.

When writing, don't be shy: despite the fact that it seems really easy to do, it isn't. There are minutes in which even expert writers have no idea what to do and get stuck, almost as if suddenly they were no longer able to control their ability to compose well. As with any other activity, practice is needed to continually improve. Notwithstanding that, of course, there is no perfect way of writing. When you can communicate your message properly, you're almost there.

A brilliant author is someone who can relate to a group of people without too many problems. It is important to focus on the content of the message we want to convey and be authentic. We should not discuss how punctuation can decisively influence the content of your speech. With the goal of focusing on the really important things, you need to improve your composing skills every day. There are some activities you can do to help you and we'll see them in a moment.

I'll ask you two questions. Do you have an idea about others based on the communication you exchange with them? Would you be able to recognize people who invest wholeheartedly in their exchanges and people who don't? Probably you'll answer YES to both questions...

In the current electronic age, one of the essential ways in which we characterize, or are defined, is through our written word. Our messages, text messages, postings via social media reveal much of our identity.

And the way we are seen from the outside affects the respect and consideration others have for you, the people around your life. These things play a significant role in your relationships, in the value you bring to others and - in the end - on the consideration you have of yourself.

17 Things to consider when writing effectively.

It truly comes down to this: do you care about how you are seen? Would you like to make a positive brand for yourself? In the event that you do, it's significant that you start investing wholeheartedly in all that you type and compose. Start today to put an accentuation on building up your composed relational abilities.

1. Write short sentences. Short sentences are easier to read through and understand than long sentences. Breaking long sentences into two assists in putting the message clearly.

2. Write in short segments, break the message body into three sentences. This assures that you will utilize the blank areas to make the message readable hence making it easy for the reader to understand what you were putting forward. Paragraphs that are tightly written are a challenge to understand. If you have to write in a tightly knitted manner, these are the advantages:

- It is efficient just as pocket-friendly.

- It gives the main topics of the message without overusing unnecessary words.

- Effective communication provides little messages that are easy to understand.

- A brief message is more engaging, conceivable, and understandable.

- A brief message is not dreary in nature.

3. Underline the primary words in each sentence.

4. Make sure to mention the reader who you intend to pass the message to so as to capture their attention and are most likely to respond to your email promptly. For example, "Greetings Eric," or "Hi Susan," tells them the message is for them and makes the individual feel respected.

5. Be straight to the point. Every message you type to make sure it is clear and mentions the important points. Everyone wants to read messages that are easy to understand once and for all. The message should be accurate in communication so that there is no syntactic blunder. Effective communication has the following qualities:

- The message is open, clear, right, and well-coordinated.

- In the event the reply is right and fast, it lifts up the confidence level.

- The correct messages to the right audience have a unique effect on them.

- Effective written communication is well structured.

- It utilizes good and correct language all through the body.

6. Try to be short and clear. Package your message in the least word count.

7. Every time you are writing, put yourself in the shoes of the reader and try to understand or look for loopholes that might hinder them from understanding it.

8. After receiving an inquiry email that is comprised of a number of questions, try as much to reply to each and every question that was asked in the best manner there is so as to effectively give fundamental feedback. This saves time as individuals will send other inquiries that you did not reply to in the previous email.

9. Number various items. On the off chance that you are answering multiple questions, break out each point utilizing numbers. I still can't seem to see a superior method to convey various points other than placing numbers before the points.

10. Utilize a cordial tone. Do you see the tone individuals pass on in their composed interchanges? Would you be able to tell when they are bothered, excessively firm, brief, or annoyed? Speaking with a benevolent tone will make you increasingly alluring, and your beneficiary progressively responsive.

11. Realize when to get the telephone. On the off chance that there is something annoying to you, get the telephone and call the other individual. Try not to enable yourself to send enthusiastic messages that can possibly scar a relationship and cause you to lament.

12. Evidence everything. Absolutely never hit the send, submit, or remark catch on anything you have not sealed. Your time the executives are never more significant than your own image.

13. Have it altered. In the event that your record is significant, go one stage past your very own sealing. Consider having somebody alter it. I have each significant archive I make altered.

14. Invest wholeheartedly. Be pleased with each message you send, including those setting off to your loved ones.

15. Completeness. The email has to start and end after replying to every issue that was at hand. The sender must figure out about the reader's outlook and pass on the message as it was intended to. Complete reverts have the following highlights:

- Complete communication makes the reputation of an organization.

- Also, they are pocket-friendly as no extra cost is acquired in passing on additional message if the communication is finished.

- A total communication consistently allows for extra data any place required. It leaves no questions unanswered.

- Complete communication assists in basic leadership by the group of beneficiaries of information as they get the vital data.

- It influences the group of spectators.

16. Consideration by putting yourself in the other person's situation. Effective communication must be able to win over the audience. Make a point to include the audience/readers' feelings and thoughts and general issues. Make sure that the respect of the reader is observed as well as the feelings are not messed up with the message that you put across. Use words and expressions that the reader will identify with as well as feel comfortable with while still sticking to the point of the whole message. Highlights of thoughtful communication include:

- Stress on the personal approach.

- Sympathize with the group of spectators and display enthusiasm for the crowd. This will ensure a positive reaction from the audience.

- Show confidence to the reader.

- Emphasize on "what is achievable" instead of "what is the dream."

- Put more weight on positive words, for example, submitted, much appreciated, warm and loved.

17. Kindness in the message gives the message a touch of care, and the reader will take it as a positive thing. The sender should be considerate, reasonable, intelligent and excited. A respectful message has the following highlights:

- Obligingness infers thinking in the same sense that the reader might comprehend the message.

- Considerate message is certain and built within society.

- It utilizes terms indicating regard for the beneficiary of the message.

- It isn't at all one-sided.

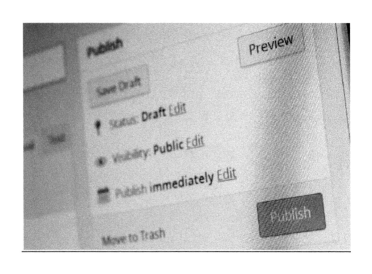

Conclusion

In this book, we explored why effective communication is important in our everyday lives as well as in organizations and for the growth of our self-esteem. In conclusion, we must continue to work the skills we have to become more fluent and skilled when communicating and understanding the society around us in order to make it better.

I thank you for coming to this point, this means that you are going to really improve your communication skills and I hope with this book that I gave you some ideas to do it.

In the field of verbal communication, we have seen what the different communication styles are, what barriers stand between us and our interlocutors and how to overcome them; we have seen how to develop effective listening and emotional intelligence.

So we got our hands dirty and we dealt with issues of everyday working life, we saw how to learn to organize and effectively manage work meetings, so that they are profitable and you get the most out of those who participate.

And even in the field of written communication, especially in writing emails, we have seen many tricks to be concise and effective, so that our messages can reach the recipients clearly and without misunderstanding.

Now don't let all this remain just something theoretical.

Instead, I would like you to commit yourself to put into practice the advice I gave you, I am sure that this will ensure that you, even if you are an introverted or shy person, will be able to develop more assertive communication skills and your communication processes will always be more a success.

And your interpersonal relationships will also improve, not only in the workplace but in a more general sense. In our time, knowing how to communicate means having power.

Final words:

Here we are… ;-)

"Effective Communication Skills" is over.

Thank you again for having read this book.

If you are serious about the will to improve your communication skills, I recommend reading this book a few times and starting to put into practice everything you have learned in this book. This way you will quickly develop better communication tactics, build trust and respect in business relationships and grow your career!

If you prefer to use the digital version to help you organize an action plan:

https://www.amazon.com/dp/B0825WYM5Q/

If you prefer to use the audiobook version, it will be available soon.

I wish you the very best of luck with the achievement of your goals!!

Did you enjoy this guide?

If you enjoyed this book, it would be awesome if you could leave a quick review on Amazon.

Your feedback is much appreciated and I would love to hear from you. ;-)

<u>Please leave a quick review on Amazon</u>

Thanks so much!!

More books by Dalton McKay:

Self-Esteem Workbook: A Practical Guide to Help You Overcome Self-Doubt and Insecurity, Gain Better Confidence, and Find Your Inner Strength. Discover Your Hidden Potential and Change Your Life in 30 Days.

More books by Dalton McKay:

Overcome Social Anxiety: A Practical Guide to Symptoms, Causes and Solutions. Discover How YOU Can Easily Cope With Panic Attacks, Phobias, and Depression and How to Improve YOUR Social Skills.

More books by Dalton McKay:

Self-Discipline Mastery. A Practical Guide to Improve YOUR Self Control, Overcome Failures, Develop Mental Toughness. Learn How to Successfully Achieve YOUR Long-Term Goals the Easy Way.

CPSIA information can be obtained
at www.ICGtesting.com
Printed in the USA
BVHW081138181120
593625BV00012B/1315